Covering Slide Mounts with Paper

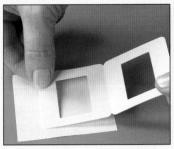

1. Glue the front of slide mount to back of paper.

2. Cut a center "X".

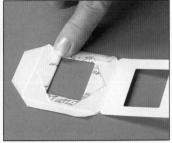

3. Miter the corners.

4. Fold the paper to the back and glue.

Collage Lovers Rejoice! Welcome to Collage Cards!

House on page 26.
Glass Slide on page 21.
Old Japan Book on page 32.
Heritage Book on page 47.
James Pin on page 30.

Creative Collage

by Carol Wingert

Collage (Fr., a pasting) an art form in which bits of objects are pasted on a surface or... fun!

Better In a Snap

Make a get well card for the seamstress in your family using buttons, snaps, and vintage papers with sewing motifs.

MATERIALS: *Design Originals* Legacy Collage Paper (#0530 Mom's Sewing Box, #0533 Dress Pattern) • *Design Originals* The Ephemera Book (#5207 p. 18) • Tan cardstock • Buttons • Snap

INSTRUCTIONS: Fold Tan cardstock to make card. Cover with Dress Pattern paper. • Sew "snap card" on collage paper. Add ruler, buttons and computer generated text printed on Dress Pattern paper.

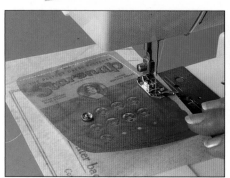  

1. Sew "Star Snap" to Collage paper. **2.** Glue on outer strips. **3.** Sew to card.

Vintage Book Box

Recycle an old gift box or use it as a template to make a new one. Gather some of your favorite things and use them to collage the box top.

MATERIALS: *Design Originals* Legacy Collage Paper (#0546 Currency) • *Design Originals* Slide Mounts (#0977 White) • *Design Originals* The Ephemera Book (#5207 p. 5) • *Art Chix Studio* watch face • *Jacquard* Brown Neopaque paint • *AMACO* ArtEmboss light Copper embossing metal sheet • *Coffee Break Design* mini brads • Lightweight posterboard • Corrugated paper • Hemp • Copy of old book spine • Folded gift box • Brown eyelet

INSTRUCTIONS: **Making Box**: Use folded gift box as template. Construct box from poster board and paint Brown. • Glue copy of book spine in place. Attach Copper strip accents on two corners with brads. • **Slide Mount:** Glue Currency paper to slide mount. Insert computer generated title printed on Currency paper. Set eyelet in slide mount corner. • **Decorating Top**: Glue Collage papers to torn corrugated paper. • Tie hemp around the papers. Tie slide mount in place. • Glue to box. Add watch face.

Fun and Games Card

Spark extra interest in game night with your group when you make this unique invitation.

MATERIALS: *Design Originals* Legacy Collage Paper (#0545 Ledger) • *Design Originals* The Ephemera Book (#5207 p. 9, 15) • Oatmeal cardstock • *Queen of Tarts* Bingo markers • *Ranger* Adirondack Brown ink • *Creative Papers Online* Lokta string • *7 Gypsies* tassels

INSTRUCTIONS: Fold Oatmeal cardstock to make card. • Glue Ledger paper to card. Lightly sponge Brown ink to age paper. • Computer generate text. Glue to card. Add vintage wooden bingo markers. • Tie string around spine. Add jewelry tassels.

Love Card

Combine embossed Silver page corners with stamped music script to convey vintage romance in this message of "LOVE".

MATERIALS: *Design Originals* Legacy Collage Paper (#0526 Two Ladies) • *Design Originals* Slide Mounts (#0977 White) • *Design Originals* Transparency Sheets (#0559 Alphabet) • Black cardstock • *Woo Hoo Wowies* heart brad • *Stampington* bendable art • *ColorBox* pigment ink • *River City Rubber Works* music stamp

INSTRUCTIONS: Fold Black cardstock to make card. • Open 2 slide mounts and lay flat. • Ink slide mounts with two shades of pigment ink. Heat set. • Lay open slide mounts side by side to create a square. Hold slide mounts steady and stamp music over the frames. • Tape letter transparencies to back of each opening. • Position slide mounts over Two Ladies paper so face shows through one opening. • Adhere slide mounts to Collage paper. • Insert decorative brad into opening where four corners meet. • Glue slide mounts to card. • Add bendable art corners and strips.

Nostalgic
by Renée Plains

Magical Delight Enchanted Joy

Looking for a fun embellishment? The slide mount on this card opens like a book, held closed by a silver clasp.

MATERIALS: *Design Originals* Legacy Collage Paper (#0547 Dictionary, #0498 TeaDye Tapestry) • *Design Originals* Slide Mount (#0977 White) • Gray cardstock • Cream text weight paper • Rubber stamps (*Stampotique Originals* words #7155V) • *ColorBox* (Alabaster fluid chalk ink pad, square moldable tip stylus) • Clear embossing ink • *Ceramcoat* Blue Haze acrylic paint • *7 Gypsies* Silver hinge • *Liberty Star* "instant relative" photo • 28 gauge Silver *Artistic Wire* • Craft knife • Coffee
INSTRUCTIONS: Paint slide frame Blue Haze. Let dry. Stamp with square moldable tip stylus using Alabaster fluid chalk ink pad. • Line inside of frame with TeaDye Tapestry paper. Cut out frame opening for front only with a craft knife. Glue photo over opening on back. Glue Dictionary paper to card. • Stamp and emboss words on Cream paper. Stain with coffee. Cut out words. Glue slide mount and words in place. • Wire and glue hinge to frame and card.

Bingo

Multiple layers give this cover dimension and interest.

MATERIALS: *Design Originals* Legacy Collage Paper (#0544 Bingo, #0490 Coffee Linen) • *Design Originals* Slide Mount (#0975 Large) • Rust cardstock • Rubber stamps (*Art Impressions* #Q-2188 star stamp; *Zettiology* "page No.") • *Ranger* Adirondacks Denim ink pad • *Ceramcoat* Sandstone acrylic paint • 1/2" heart punch • Scrap of Copper mesh • 1/8" Silver eyelet • Photo (*Jane Wynn* photo sheet) • Scrap of measuring tape • Liver of Sulphur
INSTRUCTIONS: Cut slide mount in half at hinge. Paint slide mount front with Sandstone. Let dry. Stamp star image on slide mount with Denim ink. • Glue Bingo card from Legacy paper in frame opening. Glue photo in center. • Punch a heart from aged Copper mesh. Add eyelet to heart and glue in place. (Age Copper mesh with liver of sulfur.) • Glue frame to card. Add piece of measuring tape below frame. Stamp "page No." frame on Coffee Linen and glue to card.

Believe

Send encouraging words with this very masculine looking card.

MATERIALS: *Design Originals* Legacy Collage Paper (#0551 Legacy words) • *Design Originals* Slide Mount (#0975 Large) • Tan cardstock • Parchment text weight paper • Rubber stamps (*Stampotique Originals* #7159M Otto) • *ColorBox* (Chestnut Roan Fluid Chalk ink pad, square moldable tip stylus) • *Ceramcoat* acrylic paint (Raw Sienna, Sandstone) • *Limited Edition* antique ruler stickers
INSTRUCTIONS: Paint slide mount with Raw Sienna. Let dry. Stamp with square moldable tip stylus and Chestnut Roan ink. Lightly sponge Sandstone paint. • Stamp Otto on parchment. Age with chalk. Tape to slide mount. Glue slide mount to card. • Glue ruler and "believe" under mount.

Collage

Sweet

Lacy stamps on this card match the lace on the child's gown, while aged colors create that popular nostalgic look.

MATERIALS: *Design Originals* Legacy Collage Paper (#0490 Coffee Linen, #0493 Brown Linen) • *Design Originals* Slide Mount (#0975 Large) • Cream cardstock • Cream text weight paper • Rubber stamps (*Stampotique Originals* #7109N Baroque background, #7121 border stamps; *Dawn Houser* "sweet") • *ColorBox* (Chestnut Roan Fluid Chalk ink pad, square moldable tip stylus) • *VersaMagic* Magnolia Bud ink pad • *Ceramcoat* acrylic paint (Sandstone, Raw Sienna) • *Stampa Rosa* photo sticker • 4 small eyelets

INSTRUCTIONS: Paint slide mount front with Raw Sienna. Let dry. Stamp with square moldable tip stamp and Chestnut Roan ink. Paint a wash with Sandstone on frame. • Stamp Baroque background on Coffee Linen paper with Magnolia Bud ink. Glue in frame opening. Place photo sticker in frame opening. • Add eyelets to frame corners. Glue frame to card. • Stamp border on Brown Linen paper. Cut out strip and glue under frame, trimming sides to fit. • Stamp "sweet" on Cream paper. Cut out and age with chalk. Glue in place.

Wish

Personalize your birthday message with a printed definition suitable for your subject.

MATERIALS: *Design Originals* Legacy Collage Paper (#0490 Coffee linen) • *Design Originals* Slide Mount (#0977 White) • Gold & Cream cardstock • Cream text weight paper • Rubber stamps (Star; *Stampotique Originals* "wish" definition, "wish" word; *Rubbermoon* "Birthdays are for wishing") • *Tsukineko* ink pads (Brown pigment; VersaMagic Aegean Blue, Sahara Sand) • Clear embossing powder • Brown chalk

INSTRUCTIONS: Stamp Blue stars on Coffee Linen paper. Tear paper and glue on Gold card. • Color slide mount with Sahara Sand. Tape picture in slide mount and glue to card. • Stamp "wish" definition on Cream paper. Tear paper. Age with Brown chalk. Glue in place. • Stamp "wish" on Cream cardstock and emboss with matte clear embossing powder. Stain with coffee, cut out and glue to slide mount. Stamp "Birthdays are for wishing" inside card.

Patty Cake

Create a soft nostalgic look with pastel colors and a vintage photo.

MATERIALS: *Design Originals* Legacy Collage Paper (#0535 Ruth's Letter) • *Design Originals* Slide Mount (#0977 White) • Tan cardstock • Rubber stamps (*Zettiology* label; *Rubbermoon* "patty cake") • *Tsukineko* VersaMagic Sahara Sand ink pad • Photo (*Jane Wynn* photo sheet) • Deckle scissors • Buttons

INSTRUCTIONS: Cut 3⁵/₈" x 4³/₈" piece of Ruth's Letter paper and glue to card. • Cut slide mount in half at hinge. Color slide mount with Sahara Sand ink pad. Blot and mottle ink with a crumpled paper towel. Place photo in slide mount. Glue to card. • Stamp "patty cake" on Tan paper. Glue under slide mount • Add buttons or photocopy a button card to glue under mount.

Special Occasions & Collage

by Sally Traidman

Wedding

Thank your wedding guests with a keepsake card all your friends will cherish.

MATERIALS: *Design Originals* Legacy Collage Paper (#0498 TeaDye Tapestry) • *Design Originals* Slide Mount (#0975 Large) • 4¹/2" x 6" card • *Stampington* Love, Honor, Cherish rubber stamps • Ink pads (Brown, Beige) • *Jolee's Boutique* wedding cake sticker set • 12" of ¹/4" wide sheer White ribbon • Glue dots

INSTRUCTIONS: Cover card with TeaDye Tapestry paper. • Stamp "Love", "Honor", "Cherish" in Brown ink on a 1¹/2" square of Beige paper. Age words with Brown-Beige inks. Glue to page. • Insert photo in large White slide mount. • Adhere slide mount with glue dots. Computer print names and date and attach. Weave sheer ribbon around frame. Glue flowers to ribbon and slide mount. • Attach wedding cake sticker.

Special Moments

Vintage photos are fun in more than scrapbooks. Celebrate any occasion with group photos on your cards.

MATERIALS: *Design Originals* Legacy Collage Papers (#0547 Dictionary, #0551 TeaDye Words) • *Design Originals* Slide Mount (#0978 Black) • *Design Originals* Transparency Sheet (#0556 Word Tags) • Ivory notecard • *Hero Arts* "Special Moments" rubber stamp • Brown ink pad • Deckle scissors • Gold cord

INSTRUCTIONS: Copy vintage photos. Trim edges with deckle scissors. • Cover blank card with TeaDye Words paper. Adhere "Memories" transparency near photos. • Stamp "Special Moments" in Brown onto Dictionary paper. Insert in Black photo mount. Punch hole in slide mount and attach with Gold cord. Decorate envelope to match if desired.

Life is a Journey

"A journey of a thousand miles begins with one step." This is a great sentiment for a graduation, retirement, someone starting a new business venture, or having a birthday.

MATERIALS: *Design Originals* Legacy Collage Papers (#0490 Coffee Linen, #0548 Passports) • *Design Originals* Slide Mount (#0978 Black) • *Design Originals* Transparency Sheet (#0561 Travel) • Blank Plum notecard • Tag • Jute • Rubber stamps • Postage stamps • Ephemera
INSTRUCTIONS: Mat 4 1/4" x 5 7/8" Passport paper with Coffee Linen and mount on notecard. Stamp travel related stamps in Black or Brown. Glue collage items onto card. Attach "Life is a Journey" transparency inside Black slide mount backed with Coffee Linen paper. Color back of earth on "Journey" transparency with chalk and attach to tag. Tie on twine. Glue tag to card.

About Time

Time flies when you're having fun. So, take time now to enjoy making this card with its fun watchband made from crimped paper and a slide mount.

MATERIALS: *Design Originals* Legacy Collage Papers (#0501 TeaDye Clocks, #0528 Watches) • *Design Originals* Slide Mount (#0978 Black) • *Design Originals* Transparency Sheet (#0560 Objects) • Tan cardstock • Ivory notecard • Rubber stamps (*Mostly Hearts* watches; *Hero Arts* time sayings) • Ink pads (Black, Brown) • *Jolee's Boutique* flower stickers • Gold brad
INSTRUCTIONS: Cut a 3 3/4" x 5" piece of TeaDye Clocks paper. Stamp randomly with watches and time sayings in Blacks and Browns. Mat with Tan cardstock. Glue onto Ivory notecard. • For watchband cut 1" strip of Brown corrugated. Cut watch face from Watches paper and place inside Black slide mount. Insert brad for watch stem. Glue slide mount to corrugated paper. • Attach the "time flies" transparency. Glue the watchband to the card. Randomly adhere flower stickers to card.

Dimensions in Collage

Journey Card

by Katrina Hogan

Create a sense of ocean waves with modeling paste on this slide mount. Enhance the ocean motif with sparkling fibers in aquatic colors. Aged tan cardstock looks like sand against the blue card.

MATERIALS: *Design Originals* Slide Mounts (#0975 Large) • *Design Originals* Transparency Sheet (#0561 Travel) • *JudiKins* Crackle rubber stamp • Blue and Aqua pigment inks • Tan Chalk • *Adornaments* fibers • *Liquitex* modeling paste • Cardstock (Tan, Blue) • 3/16" Blue eyelets • Spatula • Fine grit sandpaper • Sanding block

INSTRUCTIONS: **Slide mount**: Cut slide mount apart at hinge. Completely cover top of slide mount with modeling paste using spatula. Let dry. • Sponge on pigment ink for color. Punch hole for fibers using paper piercer. Tape transparency to back of slide mount. • **Textured paper:** Lightly sand Blue cardstock. • Tear Tan cardstock. Chalk edges. Dampen edges with water pen. Roll edges of paper through thumb and first finger. • **Assembly**: Glue Tan paper to the Blue card. Set eyelets. Glue slide mount in place.

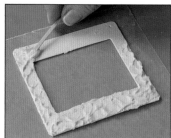

1. Apply modeling paste to slide mount. Let dry.

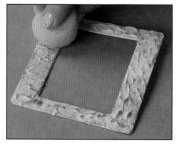

2. Ink surface to add color.

Le Jardin Des Mode
by pj dutton

This classy all-occasion card is quick and easy to make.

MATERIALS: *Design Originals* Legacy Collage Paper (#0529 Le Jardin) • *Design Originals* Slide Mount (#0977 White) • *JudiKins* Plum Tall card • Rubber Stamp (*Stampers Anonymous* #K3-715 Design Scrap) • *Brilliance* Pearlescent Sky Blue ink • Dye ink (Caribbean Blue, Grey, Deep Lilac) • Walnut ink • Paintbrush • Foam mounting tape • Pencil • Craft knife • Double-sided tape • Acetate

INSTRUCTIONS: Stamp border of card using Pearlescent Sky Blue ink. • Tear strip of Le Jardin paper. • Stipple slide mount using 3 dye inks. Stamp using Pearlescent Sky Blue. • Attach picture and acetate inside slide mount and close. • Apply foam mounting tape to back of slide mount and attach to card. • Tear name "Lady Adela" from Le Jardin paper. Paint torn edge with Walnut ink. • Attach to the slide mount with double-sided tape.

1. Press ink pad on slide mount to color.

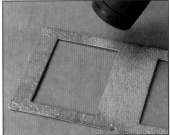

2. Emboss.

3. Sprinkle Pearl Ex.

4. Stamp with Gold while UTEE is still warm.

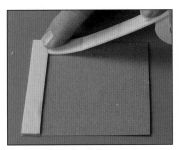

5. Apply double-stick tape to form shaker box.

6. Add beads. Place mount on top of double-stick tape.

Dad Card
by Sally Traidman

Surprise Dad with this great "Thinking of You" card. Crimped paper, twine, and metal give this card a masculine look.

MATERIALS: *Design Originals* Legacy Collage Papers (#0490 Coffee Linen, #0539 Plaid Hanky, #0553 Map) • *Design Originals* Slide Mount (#0979 Round) • *Design Originals* Transparency Sheet (#0557 Family) • Scrap of corrugated paper • 4 Gold brads • 4 Brown photo corners • Beige ink pad • Blank notecard

INSTRUCTIONS: Glue Plaid Hanky paper to blank notecard. Tear Map paper and glue to card. • Sponge slide mount with Beige ink and tape photo inside. Attach photo corners to slide mount. • Back "Dad" transparency with Coffee Linen paper and glue to crimped paper. Attach to card with brads. Glue on twine bow. Glue slide mount to card.

Dragonfly Card
by Amy Hubbard

The slide mount shaker box and layered paper give this pretty card dimension and texture.

MATERIALS: *Design Originals* Legacy Collage Paper (#0552 Travels) • *Design Originals* Slide Mount (#0975 Large) • *Design Originals* Transparency Sheet (#0562 Nature) • Blue cardstock • *Hero Arts* Italian Poetry stamp • *Ultra Thick Embossing Enamel* • *Pearl Ex* (Misty Lavender, Antique Gold) • Gold pigment ink pad • *VersaMark* stamp pad • Blue dye ink pad • *JudiKins* Diamond Glaze • Foam tape • Silver mini marbles • Glue stick • Double-stick tape • Foam tape

INSTRUCTIONS: **Slide Mount:** Paint back of dragonfly on transparency with Diamond Glaze glue. Sprinkle with glitter. Let dry. • Randomly press Blue ink pad directly onto slide mount. • Use VersaMark ink on slide mount and apply three layers of UTEE, adding Misty Lavender Pearl Ex in each layer. • While UTEE is still hot, stamp poetry on slide mount with Gold pigment ink. • Use double-stick tape to adhere transparency to slide mount. • **Shaker Box:** Trace opening of slide mount onto Blue cardstock. Align foam tape with traced opening, completely sealing the box so the beads don't leak out. Add Silver mini marbles. Remove paper from double-stick foam tape. Press top and bottom of shaker box together. • **Card Assembly:** Tear Travels paper, glue to card front. • Stamp Italian Poetry background stamp in VersaMark ink. Dust with Antique Gold Pearl Ex. • Attach shaker box to card.

Transparencies in Collage

Glittering Fishy
by Amy Hubbard

Capture the scintillating light of a goldfish bowl with torn chalked background papers and a glittered transparency painted with Diamond Glaze.

MATERIALS: *Design Originals* Slide Mount (#0975 Large) • *Design Originals* Transparency Sheet (#0562 Nature) • Cardstock (White, Green, Turquoise) • *Adornaments* Fiber • *Making Memories* page pebble • *JudiKins* Diamond Glaze • *Susie Sparkle* Winter White opaque glitter • *Hero Arts* letter stamps • Blue chalk • Green eyelets • Orange dye re-inker • Ink (Turquoise, Green) • Blue marker • Sponge • Pop dots

INSTRUCTIONS: **Transparency**: Add Orange ink to Diamond Glaze. Paint back of transparency. Sprinkle glitter. Let dry. • Chalk torn White paper. Tear Turquoise cardstock. • **Slide Mount**: Sponge slide mount with Turquoise and Green ink. • Insert transparency in slide mount. Tape torn paper behind transparency. Close slide mount. Add eyelets to slide mount. • **Card Assembly**: Draw bubbles with marker. • Stamp fishy with letter stamps. • Add page pebble over "f". • Attach slide to card with pop dots. • Tie fiber around card.

1. Drop Diamond Glaze onto the back of the transparency.   **2.** Sprinkle the glazed image area with glitter.

Framing the Fish in Style
by Judy Ross

1. Brush foam board with Duo adhesive.

This card looks more complicated than the one above, but it is surprisingly easy to make. An additional layer and new ink makes this card sparkle.

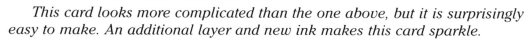

MATERIALS: *Design Originals* Legacy Paper (#0478 Green Linen) • *Design Originals* Slide Mount (#0975 Large) • *Design Originals* Transparency (#0562 Nature) • Glossy White cardstock • Foam board • Black *Memories* ink pad • E6000 • *US ArtQuest* Duo Adhesive • *LADore* Design Leaf Autumn Hue leaf foil • *Studio 2* alcohol inks (Blue Green, Light Chartreuse, Geranium Pink, Papaya) • *Wordsworth* rubber stamp • *JudiKins* Diamond Glaze • Mounting tape • Fibers • Small starfish • Craft knife • Metal ruler • Scissors • Pencil • Cutting mat • Cosmetic sponge • Foam brush

INSTRUCTIONS: Cut White cardstock 7" x 10". Score. Fold to 7" x 5". Cut Green Linen to 4$\frac{1}{2}$" x 6$\frac{1}{2}$". Stamp message. Glue to card. • Cut foam board 3$\frac{3}{4}$" x 4". **Foam Frame**: Place slide mount on foam board. Cut out opening. Brush foam board with Duo adhesive. Let dry. Apply leafing. • **Slide mount**: Cut slide mount in half at hinge. Drip 3 colors of alcohol ink on cosmetic sponge. Dab onto slide mount. Let dry. **Transparency**: Paint Diamond Glaze onto area to be colored on back of transparency. Squeeze a drop of alcohol ink onto Diamond Glaze. Let dry. • Tape transparency to back of foam board. Tape White cardstock behind transparency. Glue to card. • Adhere slide mount to foam board with 2 layers of mounting tape. • Add fibers and starfish.

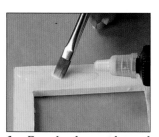

2. Apply leafing.

Illumination

by pj dutton

This classy Black and Gold card is a great example of "less is more". The elements in this card are simple, but the techniques and materials create a refined look.

1. Paint edges of slide mount with Copper.

2. Apply glue to stamp.

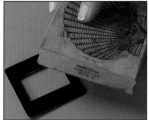

3. Stamp onto slide mount and apply leaf.

4. Remove excess foil with dry sponge.

MATERIALS: *Design Originals* Legacy Paper (#0482 Teal Stripe) • *Design Originals* Slide Mount (#0978 Black) • *Design Originals* Transparency Sheet (#0562 Nature) • *JudiKins* (Black glossy card, 2076G Shell stamp, 6804K Nature Bollio stamp) • *US ArtQuest* (Duo Embellishment Adhesive, Gildenglitz variegated gilding leaf) • Small sponge • *Cut n' Dry* foam pad • *Krylon* Leafing pens (Gold, Copper) • *Coffee Break Design* double-sided tape

INSTRUCTIONS: Edge square of Teal Stripe paper with Gold Leafing pen. • Paint White edges of slide mount with Copper leafing pen. • Squeeze Duo adhesive onto cut n' dry pad. Apply glue to Bollio stamp as you would apply ink. Stamp across bottom of card. Let dry. • Apply glue to shell stamp and stamp onto front of slide mount. Let dry. • Generously cover stamped area of card and stamped slide mount with Gildenglitz. • Press with fingers. • Shake off loose Gildenglitz. Use small dry sponge to further remove excess foil.

Faith, Hope, Love

by Shirley Rufener

Beginners, this is a card for you. Practice tinting transparencies and coloring slide mounts and make this distinctive card for a wedding, engagement, or anniversary.

MATERIALS: *Design Originals* Legacy Collage Paper (#0526 Two Ladies) • *Design Originals* Slide Mounts (#0975 Large, #0978 Black) • *Design Originals* Transparency Sheet (#0556 Word Tags) • Blue cardstock • StazOn ink pads (Blazing Red, Royal Purple, Azure) • 2 dauber applicators • 3 Fantastix applicators • Large stencil brush • Leaf adhesive • Silver leaf • Silver metallic pen • Rubbing alcohol • Fibers

INSTRUCTIONS: **Card:** Fold Blue cardstock in half for interior of card. Cut and fold Two Ladies paper to match Blue card. Use for exterior. Cut Blue cardstock smaller than Two Ladies card and glue over Two Ladies paper. • **Small Slide Mounts**: Color back of "Faith" transparency Purple. Color back of "Love" transparency Azure. Outline slide mount windows with Silver metallic pen. Insert transparencies into slide mounts. Glue slide mounts to front of card. • Punch hole in card corner. Insert fibers and knot. • **Large Slide Mount**: Apply Red ink with dauber leaving White areas. Apply Purple and Azure inks randomly. Immediately stipple with rubbing alcohol. Press and rotate brush in a spiral motion to remove some ink.• Outline slide mount window with Silver metallic pen. • **Tint Transparency**: Dot Red ink on back of "Greatest Gift" transparency with bullet applicator. Apply Purple and Azure randomly. Blend with pointed applicator. Stipple random areas on front of large transparency with leaf adhesive. When dry, apply Silver leaf sparingly. Tape "Greatest Love" transparency into slide mount. Tape slide mount closed. Secure large mount inside card with Mounting Tape.

Coloring Slide Mount

1. Apply ink leaving White areas.

2. Apply 2nd and 3rd colors. Stipple with rubbing alcohol.

3. Use brush to remove some ink.

Children are the hope of every generation. Make this treasure for your grandmother, or add it to a scrapbook page.

MATERIALS: *Design Originals* Legacy Collage Paper (#0534 Ruth's Violets, #0537 Faces of Friends) • *Design Originals* Slide Mount (#0975 Large) • *Design Originals* Transparency Sheet (#0556 Word Tags) • *JudiKins* (Ultra Crème square card, color dusters) • *Coffee Break Design* (solid head eyelets, double-sided tape) • *ColorBox* Fluid Chalk ink (Yellow Ochre, Warm Violet) • *Fiskars* 1/8" hole punch • Photo copied onto Transparency sheet • Metal label holder • *PVA* glue • Craft knife

INSTRUCTIONS: **Card base**: Stipple card edges with Yellow Ochre, then Warm Violet ink. • Tape torn Ruth's Violets paper to card. • Punch holes for metal label holder. Attach eyelets. • Cut "Hope" transparency to fit metal holder. Slide into place. • **Slide Mount**: Cover slide mount with Faces of Friends paper. Cut out window area. Carefully cut away paper around edges of slide mount. • Cut window in card so transparency photo will show through to inside. Tape photo to slide mount and close. Attach slide mount to card using double-sided tape.

Lady in Time

by pj dutton

Make a "plum perfect" birthday card that is simply elegant with vellum and vintage images.

MATERIALS: *Design Originals* Legacy Collage Paper (#0526 Two Ladies, #0528 Watches) • *Design Originals* Slide Mounts (#0979 Round) • *Design Originals* Transparency Sheet (#0560 Objects) • *JudiKins* (Plum tall card, Latte vellum, color dusters) • *Coffee Break Design* double-sided tape • *ColorBox* Fluid Chalk ink (Rose Coral, Peach Pastel, Ice Blue, Warm Violet) • *Stampers Anonymous* clock works #P1-630 rubber stamp • *Krylon* Silver leafing pen • Vellum tape

INSTRUCTIONS: **Card base**: Tape Watches paper to card front. • Cut lady from Two Ladies paper. Tape lady to vellum. Tear vellum. Tape to card. • **Slide Mount**: Cut scrap paper circle to protect window while working on slide mount. Apply Rose Coral and Peach Pastel ink to slide mount. Let dry. Stamp slide mount with Clockworks using Ice Blue ink. Sponge Rose Coral over Ice Blue. • Stamp clock image on vellum using Warm Violet ink. Tape transparency words to slide mount. • Tape vellum and transparency clock in window of slide mount and close. • Edge slide mount with Silver leafing pen. Attach to card using double-sided tape.

Salutations in Collage

Love

by Sally Traidman

Pink, hearts, diamonds, and lace romantically combine for a Valentine card, wedding invitation, or anniversary, but this beautiful card also makes a lovely "thinking of you" for someone you cherish.

MATERIALS: *Design Originals* Legacy Collage Papers (#0527 Pink Diamonds) • *Design Originals* Slide Mount (#0977 White) • *Design Originals* Transparency Sheet (#0556 Word Tags) • *Molly Jennings* heart photo • Pink cardstock • *Hero Arts* heart stamp • Pink ink pad • Heart charm • Pink ribbon • Blank notecard
INSTRUCTIONS: Glue Pink Diamonds paper to blank notecard. Crop heart photo. Mount on Pink paper. Glue to card. • Stamp slide mount with heart stamp in Pink. Insert "Love" transparency into slide mount. Glue slide mount, Pink ribbon and charm as shown.

Many Thanks

by Pam Hammons

Show your appreciation with a thoughtful thank you. Let this delicate dragonfly deliver your message in soft pastels.

MATERIALS: *Design Originals* Legacy Collage Paper (#0535 Ruth's Letter) • *Design Originals* Slide Mounts (#0975 Large) • *Design Originals* Transparency Sheet (#0562 Nature) • *Hero Arts* letter stamps • *ColorBox* Orange Fluid Chalk ink • *StazOn* Black ink • Peach organza ribbon
INSTRUCTIONS: Open slide mount. Sponge with Orange ink. Stamp "Thanks" in StazOn ink. • Tape transparency inside front of slide mount. • Cut Ruth's Letter paper to fit slide mount. Stamp images to show through back of slide mount. Glue paper inside slide mount. • Wrap ribbon around slide mount. Tie bow.

Cutting Up

by Pam Hammons

Hairdressers and hats bring ladies of fashion together. Invite your friends over for a "cut up" and make these cheerful greeting cards.

MATERIALS: *Design Originals* Legacy Collage Paper (#0531 Ladies with Hats) • *Design Originals* Slide Mounts (#0975 Large) • *Design Originals* Transparency Sheet (#0560 Objects) • *ColorBox* Fluid Chalk ink (Pink, Orange, Peach, Blue) • Gold hand charm • Variegated organza ribbon • Burgundy cardstock
INSTRUCTIONS: Open slide mount. Sponge with pastel inks. • Tape transparency inside front of slide mount. • Cut Ladies with Hats paper and cardstock to fit slide mount. Glue cardstock to paper. Glue paper to back slide mount. • Tie ribbon. Glue ribbon and charm in place.

Journey

by Pam Hammons

Jump into a pile of leaves with these two beautiful Autumn cards. Add interest with fibers and try coloring slide mounts to make your project really stand out.

MATERIALS: *Design Originals* Slide Mounts (#0977 White) • *Design Originals* Transparency Sheets (#0556 Word Tags) • Cardstock (Cream, Brown) • *Hampton Arts* stamps • *ColorBox* Cat's Eye Ink • *Adornaments* fibers • *JudiKins* Diamond Glaze
INSTRUCTIONS: **Slide mount**: Cover slide mount with Cat's Eye ink. Let dry. Cover with Diamond Glaze. Let dry. • Spread Orange ink and Diamond Glaze on back of transparency. Let dry. Back with Cream cardstock. Tape inside slide mount. Cover transparency with Diamond Glaze. Let dry. • **Card**: Make card from Brown cardstock. • Stamp oak leaf on Cream cardstock. • Cut hole for slide mount in Cream cardstock. Glue Cream cardstock to card. Glue slide mount in place.• Punch holes in corners. Thread fibers. Tape fiber ends inside card front.

Family

by Pam Hammons

MATERIALS: *Design Originals* Slide Mounts (#0977 White) • *Design Originals* Transparency Sheets (#0556 Word Tags) • Cardstock (Cream, Brown, Orange) • *Hampton Arts* stamps • *Delta* Paint Jewels • *ColorBox* Cat's Eye Ink • *Adornaments* fibers
INSTRUCTIONS: **Slide mount**: Cover slide mount with Paint Jewels. Back transparency with Orange cardstock. Tape inside slide mount. • **Card**: Make card from Brown cardstock. • Stamp oak leaf on Cream cardstock. Cut hole for slide mount in Cream cardstock. • Punch hole in corner. Thread and knot fibers. • Glue Cream cardstock to card. Glue slide mount in place.

Tea Time
by Carol Wingert

Vintage elements give this card a classical look. Add a bit of nostalgia to your next card with sewn ribbon and paper, metal brads, and old photos.

MATERIALS: *Design Originals* Legacy Paper (#0501 TeaDye Clocks) • *Design Originals* Slide Mounts (#0975 Large) • Black cardstock • *Stampington* rubber stamps • *Manto Fev* watch face • *Making Memories* (brads, letter charm) • Ink (*Ranger, StazOn, Ancient Page*) • Black ribbon

INSTRUCTIONS: Fold Black cardstock to make card. • Age Watch paper with inks. Sew Black ribbon near top. Sew Watch paper to card. Add brads and letter charm. • Sponge ink and stamp slide mount. Attach stamped image or photo inside slide mount. • Adhere slide mount to face of card with foam tape. Add stamped and aged watch face.

A Journey Begins
by Pam Hammons

Here's an alternative to gluing papers inside your cards. Fold the paper inside, punch a hole in the corner through the card and interior paper. Hold it all together with fibers. Also, check out the technique for making your transparencies glow!

MATERIALS: *Design Originals* Legacy Collage Paper (#0547 Dictionary) • *Design Originals* Slide Mounts (#0975 Large) • *Design Originals* Transparency Sheet (#0561 Travel) • Brown cardstock • Tan paper • *Hero Arts* rubber stamps • Black ink • *JudiKins* Diamond Glaze • Orange ink refill bottle • Craft tissue • *Adornaments* fibers • Embossing powder • Embossing ink

INSTRUCTIONS: Fold Brown cardstock to make card. • Stamp with Black ink. • **Slide Mount**: Open slide mount and cover front with Dictionary paper. • Cover back of transparency with Diamond Glaze. Add drops of color. Swirl a little. Crumple tissue paper and cover transparency. Let dry. • Tape transparency into slide mount. Glue slide mount to front of card. • **Tags**: Cut 2 small tags from scrap cardstock. Sponge with Orange ink. Stamp in Black ink. Emboss with clear powder. • Fold Tan paper to fit inside card. Punch hole in corner of card through inside paper. Tie fibers and tags through hole to hold paper inside card.

Booklets with Collage

Tag Pattern ◯ Punch Hole

Tag Journal
by Pam Hammons

Little books were first produced in the Middle Ages. Have fun and make a little book with pockets to store small memorabilia, love notes, or decorated slide mounts.

MATERIALS: *Design Originals* Slide Mounts (#0977 White, #0978 Black, #0979 Round) • *Design Originals* Transparency Sheet (#0556 Word Tags, #0560 Objects) • Three #1 Coin envelopes • 1 jumbo tag • Fibers • Instant coffee

Fold

INSTRUCTIONS: Stain tag and several slide mounts with coffee. (This is not an acid free technique.) Ink other slide mounts. Glue transparencies inside slide mounts. Punch hole in corner of each slide mount. Insert fibers and secure. • **Tag**: Fold tag in half. Punch holes for fibers across bottom of tag back. Attach fibers to tag from mounts. Punch larger hole in tag for fibers to tie shut. • Glue slide mount to front of book. Glue glasses transparency to slide mount. • **Accordion Envelopes**: Fold envelopes in half. Cut off ends. Glue together back to back. Do not glue all over. Leave the edges free for an accordion effect. Glue inside folded tag. Insert slide mounts in each pocket.

◯ Punch Hole

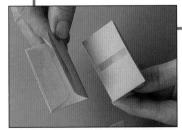

1. Tape envelopes together.

2. Tape the envelopes to the inside cover.

Camille's Wish

by Shirley Rufener

Vintage photos give character to your collage cards. The Ephemera Book offers many images to choose from. Enliven transparency images by tinting with StazOn ink.

MATERIALS: *Design Originals* Legacy Collage Paper (#0551 Legacy Words, #0488 Rust Stripe) • *Design Originals* The Ephemera Book (#5207 p. 5) • *Design Originals* Transparency Sheets (#0562 Nature) • Ivory cardstock • *StazOn* ink (Timber Brown, Royal Purple, Azure, Blazing Red, Olive Green, Mustard) • *Aleene's* Glitter & Gem glue • 6 small Gold brads • Antique Brass keyhole heart charm • Gold jump ring • Seed/bugle bead mix (Red, Gold) • No-hole Gold beads

INSTRUCTIONS: Fold cardstock in half. • Tear bottom edge of cover and color Mustard, Pumpkin, and Brown with edge of ink pad. Glue torn Legacy Words paper to card • Inside card, color bottom inch Pumpkin and Brown. • Tear girl image from The Ephemera Book. Mat with torn Rust Stripe. Glue to card. • Use StazOn ink to color tint transparency and brads. • Attach jump ring to heart charm. Secure transparency and charm to card with brads. • Apply random areas of Glitter & Gem glue and drop beads while wet.

Window to Your Dreams

by Judy Ross

Break free of traditional collage styles with this eclectic combination of colors, fibers, textures and layering.

MATERIALS: *Design Originals* Legacy Collage Paper (#0548 Passport) • *Design Originals* Slide Mounts (#0977 White) • *Design Originals* Transparency Sheets (#0556 Word Tags) • Cardstock (Black , Goldenrod) • *Memories* Black ink • *JudiKins* Diamond Glaze • *Studio 2* Ink (Caramel, Goldenrod, Ash, Flesh) • Rubber stamps (*Stampa Rosa* "Treasure"; *Limited Editions* 8775L; *Stampers Anonymous* Roman Numerals, The Rubbernecker) • Black matboard • Cosmetic sponge • 3 Gold 1/8"eyelets • 3 tags • Clock button • E6000 • Fibers (Brown, Rust) • Mounting tape • Scissors • Craft knife • Ruler • Pencil • Cutting mat

INSTRUCTIONS: Cut Goldenrod 7" x 10" and fold to make card. Stamp "Treasure" at bottom. • Cut matboard 4³/4" x 5¹/2". Mount Passport paper on matboard. Ink edges of matboard and glue to card. • Cut Black cardstock 4" x 5". Mount Passport paper on cardstock and glue to card. • **Slide mount**: Open slide mount. Sponge inks. Stamp with Black ink. Cover with Diamond Glaze. Let dry. • Apply Diamond Glaze and ink to back of transparency. Let dry. Set eyelets. **Make tags**: Sponge tags with Ash and Goldenrod inks. Stamp with Black. • Attach tags to slide mount with fibers. Tape transparency to slide mount. Foam tape slide mount to card. • Wrap fibers around inside of card at fold. Tie knot. • Add charm.

Tag Pattern

Eclectic Collage

Art Queen Greets You

by Judy Ross

It's good to be Queen! Enjoy a bit of whimsy and treat yourself to this fanciful decoration.

MATERIALS: *Design Originals* Legacy papers (#0530 Mom's Sewing Box, #0534 Ruth's Violets) • *Design Originals* Slide Mounts (#0975 Large, #0979 Round) • *Design Originals* Transparency Sheets (#0556 Word Tags, #0558 Script) • 7" x 11½" foam board • *Studio 2* inks (Lemonade, Blue violet, Flesh, Real Red) • E6000 glue • JudiKins Diamond Glaze • Black *Memories* ink pad • StazOn Black ink pad • Rubber stamps (*Stampers Anonymous* M2-887 and Imagine; *Catslife Press* Art Doll, Character Constructions Legs and Arms, *Stamp Francisco* saying) • Acetate • White card stock • Scissors • Ruler • Pencil • Craft knife • Cutting mat • 2 Gold clipolas • 2 heart charms • 2 Gold crystals • Doll hair • Cosmetic sponges

INSTRUCTIONS: **Large Slide Mount:** Drip 3 colors alcohol ink onto cosmetic sponge. Dab onto slide mount and back of Script transparency. Let dry. • Stamp slide mount with Memories ink. • Glue "Inspire" transparency to "Script" transparency with Diamond Glaze. • Glue transparency to torn Ruth's Violets paper with Diamond Glaze. • Tape into slide mount. • **Doll Parts:** Stamped doll parts must be cut out with margin around pieces. Stamp art doll twice onto acetate with StazOn ink.• Drip alcohol ink onto cosmetic sponge. Dab on back of face and slide mount. Let dry. • Tape face in slide mount. Glue crown, hair and crystals to slide mount. Glue head piece to large slide mount. • Roughly cut out acetate arms and legs. Glue to Mom's Sewing Box paper. Glue to cardstock. Cut out. Glue to body. Glue clips and charms in place. **Assembly:** Tear strips from Mom's Sewing Box. Glue to foam board. • Stamp "All I ask" onto foam board with StazOn ink. • Glue Art queen to foam core board.

All I ask is that you treat me no differently than you would the Queen

1. Dab the inks on the slide mounts with brush.

2. Stamp large slide mount.

3. Glue transparencies.

4. Choose the paper background for body.

Dawn
by Cindy Pestka

Looking for a unique room decoration? Make a slide mount mobile with your name. Choose papers and ephemera to match your personality.

MATERIALS: *Design Originals* Legacy Collage Paper (#0547 Dictionary, #0555 Tags, #0497 TeaDye Letters, #0411 Letter Postcards) • *Design Originals* Slide Mounts (#0975 Large) • *Design Originals* Transparency Sheets (#0559 Alphabet) • Acrylic paint (Blue, Gold) • Acetate • Dried flowers • White glue • Beading thread • Assorted beads • Copper wire for hanger

INSTRUCTIONS: **Prepare slide mounts**: Paint slide mounts with Blue and Gold acrylic paint. • Cut 2 pieces of acetate for each slide mount. • Layer paper, transparency letter, and dried flowers between acetate sheets. Glue in place. • Glue transparency sandwich into slide mount. Punch holes at top and bottom of each slide mount as shown. • **Connect slide mounts**: Cut 5" lengths of beading thread. Add 1" of beads. String top slide mount to the one below it. Knot thread and trim. • Add wire hanger to top slide mount. Decorate bottom slide mount with strings of beads.

Night Light
by Babette Cox

Is there a space in your home that needs extra light? Illuminate it with this elegant night light.

MATERIALS: *Design Originals* Slide Mount (#0975 Large) • *Design Originals* The Ephemera Book (#5207 p. 26, 29) • *RO-DAF* wooden teabags box • *Craftware* no hole glass beads (Dark Blue/Red/Purple blend) • Red Liner tape • *Aleene's* Tacky Glue • Leafy floral wire • White paper • Transparency film for inkjet copiers • *Lasting Impressions* stencil • Light Green velvet paper • Hot glue • Wooden beads • Gold leaf • Adhesive sizing • Small light on electric cord • Drill • Blue painters tape • *DAP* Fast 'N Final Lightweight Spackling

INSTRUCTIONS: Drill hole in box lid for bulb. Drill hole in bottom of box for cord to come out. • Secure light in box. • Position transparency on box lid, folding it so part is on box lid and part is standing up. • Clip bottom of transparency so it bends slightly. • Apply Red Liner tape to sides and top of box, leaving hole for light. • Dip box in bowl of colored beads to cover. • Glue 2 slide mounts to back side of velvet paper. Cut out window area. • Tape stencil over velvet paper. Apply spackle. Remove tape, lift stencil straight up right away. Clean stencil immediately. Let dry. • Make transparencies of images from The Ephemera Book. Tape images to back of slide mounts. Curve pictures and slide mounts slightly. Glue White paper to back. • Hot glue transparency/velvet/picture sandwich to box's transparency sheet that is standing up. • Hot glue leafy floral wire. • Put leaf adhesive on wooden beads. Apply Gold leaf. Let dry. • Hot glue feet to box. • Sign your work.

Art Is a Journey
by Shirley Rufener

Give a new look to an old frame plus display your creative slide mount art.

photo on page 21

MATERIALS:
Design Originals Legacy Collage Paper (#0552 Travels, #0554 Diamonds, #0487 Rust Linen) • *Design Originals* Slide Mounts (#0977 White, #0978 Black, #0979 Round) • *Design Originals* Transparency Sheets (#0556 Word Tags) • Cardstock • Large White letter beads (I, S, A) • Wire (8" Bronze 22 gauge, 60" Copper 26 gauge) • *Anita's* two-step Fragile Crackle medium • *Aleene's* (Memory Glue, Quick Dry Tacky Glue, Instant Decoupage medium) • *StazOn* ink pads (Mustard, Olive Green, Timber Brown, Pumpkin) • *Xyron* Adhesive Runner • *Fantastix* applicators (bullet, pointed) • ¹/₁₆" hole punch • Adhesive foam dots • Open wood frame

Punch ¹/₁₆" holes in the corners with a paper punch.

INSTRUCTIONS:
Frame: Cover frame with Travels paper using Decoupage medium. Let dry. • Apply Fragile Crackle step one. Let dry. Apply step two. • Antique details by applying Brown glaze and wiping excess with lint-free cloth. • Wrap 10" pieces of Copper wire around corners. • Glue Rust Linen paper to cardstock. Cut to frame size. Attach with Adhesive Runner. • **Slide Mounts**: Color tint "ART" transparency with Mustard, Pumpkin and Brown ink. Color round slide mount with Mustard with a hint of Green. Age edges with Brown ink. • Place Diamonds paper behind ART transparency. Align in window of round mount.

Layer map area of Travels paper inside Black slide mount. Add aged letter beads with Copper wire. • Glue Travels paper on square White slide mount. Age edges with Brown ink. Layer floral area of Travels paper inside slide mount and tape "Journey" transparency at an angle. • **Link Slide Mounts**: Punch holes in slide mounts. Add Bronze wire links. Secure slide mounts to background with foam dots.

Collage with a Twist

Adventure
by Cindy Pestka

Collage paper and transparencies inside glass slides to make a fun wall hanging.

1. Put a rubber band around slides.

2. Twist wire ends together.

MATERIALS: *Design Originals* Legacy Collage Paper (#0534 Ruth's Violets, #0537 Faces of Friends, #0539 Plaid Hanky, #0548 Passport, #0411 Letter Postcards) • *Design Originals* Transparency Sheet (#0556 Word Tags) • Glass microscope slides • 48" of 22 gauge wire • White glue

INSTRUCTIONS: Glue papers together. Add a transparency word. Place it between 2 glass slides. • Cut two 24" lengths of wire. Bend in half. • Place slide in the bend. Twist wire as though closing a twist tie. • Twist wires for an inch. Open wires. Place next slide in place. Twist wire again. Continue until all slides are connected. • About 5" from the top slide, twist the wires together to make a hanger loop.

Covering Mounts	Tinting Transparencies	Layering Mounts	Connecting Mounts	Accenting with Wire

1. Trace and cut out paper.	**1.** Dot ink on back of transparency.	**1.** Dot color with bullet applicator.	**1.** Wrap wire around 2 jig pegs.	**1.** Thread ink-aged beads on the wire.
	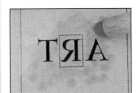		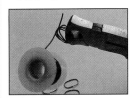	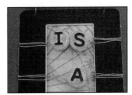
2. Spread Memory Glue. Secure paper.	**2.** Add additional colors if desired.	**2.** Glue paper inside slide mount.	**2.** Clip 1 side of wire ovals to make links.	**2.** Wrap wire around slide mount.
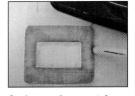	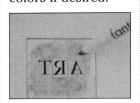			
3. Age edges with Brown StazOn ink.	**3.** Blend colors with pointed applicator.	**3.** Tape or glue transparency behind window.	**3.** Punch 1/16" holes. Insert links. Close with pliers.	**3.** Wrap wire around corners of the frame.

Slide Mounts Fibers and Tags

Fuzzy Brag Book

by Shirley Rufener

Fibers and shiny embellishments make this fuzzy book fun to touch. Show off your child or grandchild with this great Brag book.

MATERIALS: *Design Originals* Slide Mount (#0975 Large) • *Aleene's* (Patch & Applique glue, Glitter & Gem glue) • *StazOn* ink pads (Blazing Red, Ultramarine, Royal Purple, Hunter Green, Olive Green, Pumpkin) • 6 dauber applicators • Rubbing alcohol, 18" Purple 22 gauge wire • 2 yds fuzzy fibers • 8 rhinestones • 6 acrylic mirrors • 1/8" hole punch • Large stencil brush • Wire cutters • Mounting tape • Photos

INSTRUCTIONS: Mark dots every 1/4" on slide mount and punch 1/8" holes for spiral hinge. Note: you may wish some mounts to have horizontal windows. • Using ink colors to coordinate with photos, apply ink to slide mounts with dauber leaving White areas. Apply second and third color randomly. Immediately stipple with rubbing alcohol. Press and rotate brush in a spiral motion to remove some ink. Let dry. • Tape photos back to back with mounting tape. Insert into slide mounts. Tape slide mounts shut. • Wrap an 18" piece of 22 gauge wire around a 1/4" cylinder. Stack slide mount pages. Twist wire to thread spiral. • Apply a line of Patch & Applique glue 1/8" from window and secure fibers. Embellish with rhinestones and mirrors using Gem glue.

Make this delightful fuzzy book of love!

1. Punch 1/8" holes in slide mount every 1/4".

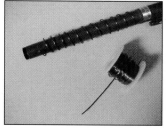

2. Wrap the wire around a 1/4" cylinder.

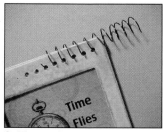

3. Twist the wire to thread the spiral.

Baby Brent

by Sally Traidman

Stamped symbols in baby pastels make this card fun. Make tags for boys in blue, for girls in pink. Quick and easy, this announcement gives the birth of a baby the attentions it deserves.

MATERIALS: *Design Originals* Slide Mount (#0977 White) • *Design Originals* Transparency Sheet (#0557 Family) • White notecard • Scrap of Blue dot paper • *Hero Arts* Baby rubber stamps • Ink pads (Blue, Pink) • Light Blue tag • 2 Blue star buttons • 8" Blue ribbon

INSTRUCTIONS: Stamp Blue and Pink baby stamps randomly over White card. • Adhere "Baby" transparency to Blue dot paper. Glue to tag. • Enclose baby photo in slide mount. Glue to tag. Add ribbon to tag. Attach tag to card. • Computer print name and date. Glue to slide mount. • Attach tiny buttons.

Oh Baby!

by Mary Kaye Seckler

Announce your new arrival with a slide mount shaker box covered in silk ribbon. Finish your tag with matching fibers.

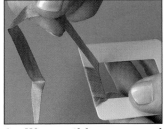

1. Wrap ribbon around slide mount.

2. Add buttons. Remove paper from foam tape.

MATERIALS: *Design Originals* Slide Mounts (#0977 White) • *Design Originals* Transparency Sheet (#0557 Family) • *Bucilla* variegated silk ribbon • *Karen Foster Design* buttons • *Stamping Station* fold over tags • *On the Surface* fibers • *Hero Arts* Playful Upper and Lowercase alphabet stamps • Ink (*ColorBox* Cat's Eye Colonial Blue, Old Rose; *Printworks* Yorktown Blue, Raspberry Pink) • Red Liner Tape • 2 pieces acetate • *3M* double-stick mounting tape

INSTRUCTIONS: Cut slide mount in half. • Line reverse side of one half with Red Line tape. Wrap ribbon around slide mount. Affix transparency with Red Liner Tape. Add double-stick tape in a complete square over transparency. (If tape is not complete, buttons will leak out.) Sprinkle buttons inside mounting tape. Stipple other half of slide with matching dye ink. Affix acetate with Red Line Tape. Attach back half of slide mount to front. Attach slide to front of tag. • Add fibers.

When you display or give these decorative plaques, everyone will want to know where you bought them. Make these specialty store accents for a fraction of the price in a style and color that is uniquely yours.

Home Decor and Collage

BASIC MATERIALS: *Walnut Hollow* 5" x 7" thin wood plaque • Thin corrugated board 5" x 7" • Double-sided tape • *PVA* glue • Glue brush • Hammer • Screw driver • 1 large nail • Drill • Wire nipper • Gold 2" x 8/32" machine screw with 2 nuts for frame stand

INSTRUCTIONS: FRAME COVER: Cut 8" x 10" base paper. Glue to front of plaque. Do not glue edges yet. • Miter corners(see diagram) and glue long side first then short ends. • Decorate frame. • Prepare slide mounts. • Attach slide mounts and embellishments

FRAME STAND: (See frame back photo) • Drill hole for screw at center and 1 inch from bottom. Screw will be frame stand. • Glue corrugated paper to back of plaque. • Use a nail to poke screw hole through backing board. • Slide washer on screw and tighten into place. The first nut will screw tightly to back of plaque and second nut will stay at end of screw to prevent scratching your table.

Miter Paper Corners

Cut C Cut B Cut A Paper **Wood** Paper Paper	Cut A - even with the edge of the wood Cut B - equals the thickness of the wood Cut C - a miter cut

Home
by pj dutton

MATERIALS: *Design Originals* Legacy Collage Paper (#0541 Report Card, #0542 Father's Farm) • *Design Originals* Slide Mount (#0975 Large) • *Design Originals* Transparency Sheet (#0556 Word Tags) • Family photo • Craft knife • Hole punch • 1 rubber washer • 4 upholstery tacks

INSTRUCTIONS: Follow Frame Cover instructions using Report Card paper. • Glue torn Father's Farm paper on plaque. • Cover slide mount with Father's Farm paper. Remove paper at center of slide mount with craft knife. • Tape photo inside slide mount. • Glue slide mount shut. • Position slide mount on plaque and hammer tacks at each corner. Cut ends of tack with wire nippers if they come through back. • Cut out "HOME" transparency and punch hole at lower center. • Follow directions for Frame stand. Slide washer on screw before transparency.

Bon Jour
by pj dutton

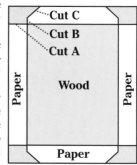

MATERIALS: *Design Originals* Legacy Collage Paper (#0553 Map, #0485 Blue Stripe, #0486 Blue Floral) • *Design Originals* Slide Mount (#0975 Large) • *Design Originals* Transparency Sheet (#0561 Travel) • *Krylon* Copper leafing pen • *Coffee Break Design* 1" Incredi-tape • *US Art Quest* (Duo Embellishment Adhesive , Gildenglitz foil) • Family photo • Fleur de lis Brass charm • Gold 8/32" round head machine screws (One 2 inch long, Three 3/4" long) • 4 nuts • Washers (3 Copper 5/8", 3 Gold 1/2", 3 Silver 3/8") • Super glue • Paintbrush

INSTRUCTIONS: Follow Frame Cover instructions using Blue Floral paper. • Cut Blue Stripe paper 2" x 8". Cut Map paper 1 1/4" x 8". Mat Map paper on center of Blue Stripe. Edge Blue Stripe and Map papers with Krylon marker. • Glue to plaque. • Use double-sided tape to apply leafing foil to Map paper. • Glue charm top center with super glue. • **Slide Mount:** Edge slide mount with Krylon pen. Paint front of slide mount with Duo Embellishment Adhesive glue. Let dry. Apply leafing foil. • Tape transparency and Map paper inside slide mount. Position on plaque. Mark drill holes. Drill 2 holes to hold slide mount to frame. Stack washers on screws. Screw slide mount in place. • Follow directions for Frame stand.

Hope, Dream, Believe

by pj dutton

Beautify your home with unique accents that reflect your personality. Flowers fit into any decor. Let this cheery flower holder brighten your room!

MATERIALS: *Design Originals* Heritage Paper (#0414 Roses and Letters) • *Design Originals* Slide Mounts (#0977 White) • *Making Memories* word eyelets • *US ArtQuest* (Duo Embellishment Adhesive, Gildenglitz foil) • *JudiKins* #2528H pressed fern rubber stamp • *Ranger* Cut n' Dry foam pad • Family photo • 3 Gold 3/4" long 8/32" round head machine screws with nuts • Washers (4 Copper 5/8", 4 Gold 1/2", 4 Silver 3/8") • Walnut ink • Paintbrush

Tip: When stamping glue, wash stamp immediately. Do not let glue dry on stamp.

INSTRUCTIONS: Follow Frame Cover instructions using Roses and Letters paper. • Paint slide mounts with Walnut ink. Dab with paper towel while wet to mottle ink. Let dry. • Squeeze Duo embellishment adhesive onto cut n' dry foam. Use as stamp pad to apply glue to stamp. Stamp slide mounts and frame with fern stamp. Let dry to clear. • Pour foil on stamped areas. Press with fingers. Brush away excess. • Tape photos inside slide mounts and close. • Paint slide mount edges with Walnut ink. • Position slide mounts and words on plaque. • Mark holes for drilling. • Drill holes and glue word eyelets in place. • Follow directions for Frame stand.

Tussy Pattern

Tussy Mussy

by Cindy Pestka

MATERIALS: *Design Originals* Legacy Collage Paper (#0534 Ruth's Violets) • Cardstock • Double-stick tape • Hole punch • Silk flowers • Hot glue gun • Ribbons • Blue Cotton Perle • Hanger wire • Sturdy cardboard • Scissors

INSTRUCTIONS: Glue Ruth's Violets paper to cardstock. Cut out cone using template. Curl paper into cone shape. Tape edges • Punch 2 holes on opposite sides of top. Thread wire for hanger. • Hot glue silk flowers to top and sides of cone. • Tie ribbons from hanger. **Make tassel:** Cut cardboard 2" x 4". Wrap thread 50-100 times around width. • Slide 12" length of thread under wound fiber and tie tightly. Tie 12" tails together. On cardboard opposite tie, cut yarn apart with scissors. Trim ends even. • Thread 12" tails through hole in bottom of cone. Pull taut. Tape to inside of cone. • Stuff with tissue paper to maintain shape. Add flowers.

1. Wrap the thread 50-100 times around width.

2. Tie off tightly.

3. Cut the threads apart. Trim the ends even for tassel.

Creating a home is still the great American dream. This house contains all the things we hope for . . . treasured memories, precious moments, beauty, and charming friends.

1. Cut strip.

2. Remove plastic.

3. Sponge paint slide.

4. Color words with Coffee.

MATERIALS: *Design Originals* Legacy Paper (#0489 Rust Floral, #0493 Brown Linen, #0498 TeaDye Tapestry) • *Design Originals* Slide Mounts (#0979 Round) • Cream text weight paper • 10" x 14" matboard • Rubber stamps (*Stampotique Originals* #7121K border stamp, #7155V words, #7167V tall words; *Uptown Design* Baroque Crest #E31031) • *Tsukineko* VersaMagic Magnolia Bud ink pad • Embossing ink • Brown chalk • *Nostalgiques* ruler stickers • *Ceramcoat* Sandstone acrylic paint • *Jane Wynn* photo sheet • ⁵⁄₈" heart charm • Craft knife • Instant coffee

INSTRUCTIONS: Cut house from matboard using diagram. Glue 8¹⁄₂" x 8¹⁄₂" Tapestry paper centered at bottom of house. Glue Rust paper on roof. Trim roof edges from back with craft knife. Stamp border on Brown linen four times with Magnolia Bud ink. • Cut ¹⁄₂" strips and glue to edges of matboard covering Tapestry edge. Place ruler stickers on roof. • Stamp Baroque crest on Brown linen with Magnolia Bud ink. Cut out. Glue to roof. Glue a heart charm to crest. • Paint round slide mounts with Sandstone. • Let dry. Age edges with chalk. • Stamp and emboss words on Cream paper. • Mix coffee crystals with a little warm water. Stain with coffee. • Cut words out. Glue to slide mounts. Glue photo in slide mount. Glue slide mounts to house. • Stamp "Dare to Dream" on Brown Linen paper with Brown ink and emboss. Cut out. Glue to roof.

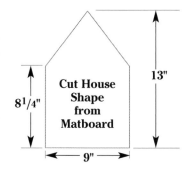

Cut House Shape from Matboard

8¹⁄₄"   9"   13"

Families & Dreams in Collage

Mom

by Shari Carroll

Collage projects can be small. This is a great one for beginners or children. Recycle an old frame, collage the inside, and add embellishments for a very designer boutique look you made yourself.

MATERIALS: *Design Originals* Legacy Collage Papers (#0526 Two Ladies, #0530 Mom's Sewing Box, #0546 Currency, #0547 Dictionary) • *Design Originals* Slide Mount (#0978 Black) • *Hero Arts* Rubber Stamps • *Memories* dye ink • Uchida hole punch • *Rollabind* Silver discs • Frame

INSTRUCTIONS: Collage papers to fit inside frame. Stamp flowers and words. Place under frame glass. • Stamp "mom" letters with Black ink. Punch out with 1/2" hole punch. Glue to disc. Attach letters to frame glass. • Open slide mount. Wrap fiber around each side. Insert photo. Close slide-mount. Glue to frame glass. Wrap fiber around frame. Tie knot in front.

Little Girl In Frame

by Babette Cox

When you find a photo that makes you smile, display it where you will see it often. This happy little girl is just one of many images to be found in The Ephemera Book.

MATERIALS: *Design Originals* Legacy Collage Paper (#0547 Dictionary, #0491 Coffee Stripe) • *Design Originals* Slide Mounts (#0977 White) • *Design Originals* Transparency Sheets (#0556 Word tags, #0557 Family) • *Design Originals* The Ephemera Book (#5207 p. 7) • 4" x 6" self-standing glass frame • Hot glue • Charms • Fiber • *Aleene's* Tacky Glue

INSTRUCTIONS: **Slide Mounts**: Cover 3 slide mounts with Dictionary paper. Glue transparencies behind windows. Tie fiber to charm. Hot glue in place. Cover back with Coffee Stripe, with stripes going vertically. • **Frame**: Cut Coffee Stripe to fit frame, with horizontal stripe. Cut opening for image from The Ephemera Book. • Lightly glue to back of picture stand. • Attach slide mount and charm with hot glue. • Sign your work.

Timeless Treasures

1. Run cut-outs through Xyron.

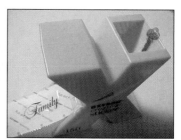
2. Run transparency through Xyron.

Jeweled Coin Box
by Cindy Pestka

Add sparkle to vintage paper with rhinestones when you make this box. Decorate several for gifts.

MATERIALS: *Design Originals* Legacy Collage (#0546 Currency, #0550 TeaDye Script, #0552 Travels, #0483 Teal Floral) • *Design Originals* Slide Mount (#0979 Round) • Gold spray paint • *Brilliance* ink • White glue • Awl • Wire • Rhinestones • Tin box • Coin • Mounting tape
INSTRUCTIONS: Spray tin with Gold. Glue paper to inside lid and bottom. Collage paper to cover. • **Slide Mount:** Ink slide mount. • Poke holes with awl. • Glue coin inside slide mount. • Coil wire through holes. • Glue feather and slide mount into bottom of box. • Glue rhinestones to peacock feathers.

Family Time Frame
by Shirley Rufener

We all love "family time"- those special moments spent together without distractions from our frenzied lives. Display those special times in this heir-loom frame.

MATERIALS: *Design Originals* Legacy Papers (#0501 TeaDye Clocks, #0411 Letter Postcards) • *Design Originals* Slide Mounts (#0975 Large) • *Design Originals* Transparency Sheets (#0560 Objects, #0556 Word Tags) • Old photos • *Xyron* (150 Create-A-Sticker, 510 with Permanent Adhesive, Solutions Adhesive Runner) • *StazOn* Black ink • *Brilliance* ink pads (Cosmic Copper, Galaxy Gold) • 2 dauber applicators • *Aleene's* (7800 Adhesive, Memory Glue) • Black tassel • Old buttons • Adhesive Sizing • Gold leaf sheet • Deckle edge scissors • Two-photo frame
INSTRUCTIONS: **Slide Mounts:** Apply Black ink. Age edges with Copper ink using dauber. Stipple random areas with adhesive sizing. Add Gold leaf sparingly. • **Transparencies:** Cut "Family" and "Time" with deckle scissors. Apply adhesive sizing to back. Let dry. Add Gold leaf. • **Frame:** Decorate frame randomly with Gold and Copper ink using daubers. • Glue Clocks paper to frame insert. • Run Postcard paper through Xyron. Adhere to frame at angles. • Make transparency stickers. Adhere over Postcard designs. Secure photos in slides with Adhesive Runner. Glue leafed words in place. Secure slide mounts, tassel and buttons with 7800.

in Collage

Designer Clock
by Cindy Pestka

Old vinyl record albums make great clocks. Consider game pieces, charms, flat glass marbles, silk petals, or leaves when choosing the embellishment for clock numbers. Make your clock distinctly yours.

MATERIALS: *Design Originals* Legacy Collage Paper (#0542 Father's Farm) • Plastic disk with center hole • E6000 glue • Vintage buttons • Clock mechanism • Clock hands
INSTRUCTIONS: Glue Father's Farm paper to disk. Add the cropped photos and buttons. • Insert the clock mechanism through the hole in center and attach the hands.

Book Marks
by Cindy Pestka

Bookmarks make great gifts. Add an interesting twist with a transparency window. Remember, these simple projects are great to do with kids!

1. Cut out window.

2. Add photo corners.

MATERIALS: *Design Originals* Legacy Collage Papers (#0528 Watches, #0530 Mom's Sewing Box, #0532 Red Patterns, #0549 Shorthand) • *Design Originals* The Ephemera Book (#5207 p. 7, 37) • *Design Originals* Slide Mount (#0977 White) • *Design Originals* Transparency Sheets (#0556 Word Tags, #0557 Family) • Cardstock • Scissors • Glue • Fibers • Eyelets • Mica • Tag • Button • Ink (*Ancient Page, Brilliance*)
INSTRUCTIONS: Cut 2 pieces cardstock 2½" x 7". Cut window in both. • Tape transparency in window. • Glue cardstock pieces together. • Collage front and back. • Punch hole in top. Add fibers. • **Tag Bookmark:** Sponge tag with ink. • Open 1 slide mount. Decorate it. • Place transparency behind slide mount openings. Cover openings with mica. Attach mica with eyelets. • Glue slide mount to bookmark. • Add button to top. • The Purple bookmark is also made from a tag. • Follow directions for tag bookmark. Add photo corners to slide mounts. Glue to tag.

James Pin
by Mary Kaye Seckler

Antique brass charms give a quality reminiscent of Grandmother's jewelry box in these unique fashion pins.

MATERIALS: *Design Originals* The Ephemera Book (#5207, p. 15) • *Design Originals* Slide Mount (#0977 White), *Fancifuls* (filigree, watch charm) • *Limited Edition* miniature game pieces • Antique photo • Clear acetate • Red Liner Tape • *ColorBox* Cat's Eye ink pads(Rose, Chestnut) • Pin back • 1/16" hole punch

INSTRUCTIONS: Open slide mount. Cover front of slide mount with image from The Ephemera Book. Cut "x" in slide opening. Wrap paper to inside of slide mount. Tape in place. • Tape photo and acetate inside slide mount. Tape shut. • Wrap outside edges of image from The Ephemera Book around slide and tape into place. Edge with Rose ink, followed by Chestnut ink to age. • Age 'James' letters with Chestnut ink. Glue on frame. Punch 1/16" hole for jump ring in slide mount. Glue Brass filigree to slide mount. Slide jump ring through hole and add watch charm. • Glue pin to back.

Lily Pin
by Mary Kaye Seckler

MATERIALS: *Design Originals* The Ephemera Book (#5207, p. 6) • *Design Originals* Slide Mount (#0977 White) • Brass jump ring • *Fancifuls* (filigree, heart charm) • *Limited Edition* miniature game pieces • *Hero Arts* rubber stamp • Copper acrylic paint • Black *Memories* ink pad • Red liner tape • *ColorBox* Chestnut Cat's Eye • Pin back • Glue dots • 1/16" hole punch

INSTRUCTIONS: Paint front of slide mount in 2 coats Copper paint. Let dry. • Stamp in Black. Tape child's picture into slide mount. • Affix brass filigree with glue dots. • Age 'Lily' letters with Chestnut Ink. Glue to frame. • Punch 1/16" hole. Attach Brass heart charm with jump ring. • Glue pin back on reverse side.

1. Attach image to front of slide mount. **2.** Cut "x" inside opening. Wrap tabs to inside.

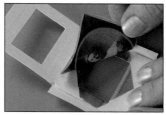 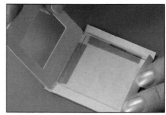

3. Attach the photo and the acetate. **4.** Apply Red Liner tape. Wrap outside edges back.

Glass Magnets
by Cindy Pestka

Hold notes to your refrigerator in style with these easy to make glass marble magnets. Draw attention to those very important messages with a Roaring 20's beaded fringe magnet.

MATERIALS: *Design Originals* Legacy Collage Paper (#0546 Currency, #0552 Travels) • *Design Originals* The Ephemera Book (#5207, p. 19, 29) • E6000 • White glue • Magnets • Glass marbles
INSTRUCTIONS: Use White glue to stick bits of paper to flat side of clear marbles. Let dry overnight. • Affix magnets with E6000.

Fun Refrigerator Magnet
by Babette Cox

MATERIALS: *Design Originals* The Ephemera Book (#5207 p. 20) • *Design Originals* Slide Mount (#0975 Large, #0977 White) • Sponge brush • Brown acrylic paint • *AMACO* (Copper WireForm mesh, Gold Rub 'n Buff) • Amber Chrome nail polish • Gold *Krylon* pen • Bead fringe • Brass stencil • *DAP* Spackling paste • *Aleene's* Tacky glue • Hot glue • Magnet • Paper scraps
INSTRUCTIONS: Paint both slide mounts with Brown acrylic paint using sponge brush. Let dry. • Edge slide mounts with Gold pen. • Apply spackle through Brass stencil to smaller slide mount. Let dry. • Rub spackle with Gold Rub 'n Buff • Glue beaded fringe to bottom of smaller slide with hot glue. • Paint Copper mesh with Amber Chrome nail polish. Let dry. • Write on paper scrap cut in strips. Glue to large slide mount. • Insert image from The Ephemera Book in small slide mount. Use skirt from same image for large slide mount. • Hot glue all pieces together. • Glue magnet to back. • Sign your work.

Collage Fun

Door Style Cards

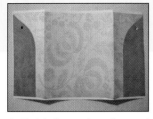

1. Fold the side edges of cardstock to the center. Cover outside of card with printed paper.

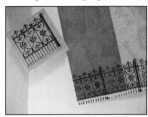

2. Add door print. Chalk door and card edges.

3. Stamp images.

Beaded Fringe

1. Glue trim to inside cover of slide mount.

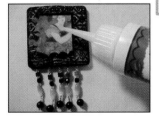

2. Glue image. Apply paper glaze.

3. Glue velvet paper to back. Adhere pin back with 7800.

Jewelry Container

by Cindy Pestka

MATERIALS: *Design Originals* Legacy Collage Paper (#0537 Faces of Friends) • *Design Originals* Transparency Sheet (#0561 Travel) • Round tin • Decorative trim • Rhinestone • Glue

INSTRUCTIONS: Cut Faces of Friends paper to fit the bottom of the container. Glue in place. • Attach transparency inside container lid. • Glue rhinestone to lid. • Glue trim around outside of container.

2. Apply thin layer of Clear Gel Tacky glue to front surface.

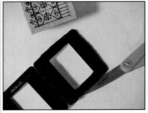

4. Stamp clay. Trim overlap with scissors.

Door Pattern

Textured Slide Mounts

1. Ink the edges to match the clay.

3. Roll air dry clay to 1/16" thick. Secure to slide mount.

5. Rub surface with metallic paste wax.

Textured Pin Gift Card

by Shirley Rufener

MATERIALS: *Design Originals* Legacy Paper (#0489 Rust Floral, #0498 TeaDye Tapestry) • *Design Originals* Slide Mounts (#0978 Black) • *Design Originals* The Ephemera Book (# 5207 p. 21) • Tan cardstock • *Stampendous* (sm. wrought iron gate, ivy rubber stamp) • Dye ink pads (Black, Olive Green, Leaf Green) • Air-dry Black clay • Adhesive Runner • Brown chalk • Beaded trim • *Aleene's* (Clear Gel Tacky Glue, Paper Glaze, 7800 All-Purpose Adhesive) • Flat paintbrush • Metallic Silver paste wax • Black velvet paper • 1¼" long Silver bar pin back • ¼" hole punch

INSTRUCTIONS: Fold side edges of cardstock to center. • Cover card with TeaDye Tapestry paper leaving ¼" border. Cut two halves of door from Rust Floral paper. Tape doors to card with Adhesive Runner. Age edges with Brown chalk. • Stamp two-tone Green ivy along sides of door and bottom card edge. Stamp Black gate along bottom edge. Make lady image slide pin according to "Textured Slide Mount" and "Beaded Fringe" directions on this page. Clip around hair detail and allow to overlap frame. Squeeze Paper Glaze over image, but brush it onto clay to retain texture. Press pin back onto card to impress pin position. Punch holes over marks. Secure pin to card through holes to close card.

Dragonfly Pin

by Shirley Rufener

This jeweled dragonfly pin glitters with natural textures.

MATERIALS: *Design Originals* Slide Mounts (#0978 Black) • *Design Originals* Transparency Sheet (#0562 Nature) • *StazOn* ink pads (Pumpkin, Timber Brown) • *Fantastix* bullet and pointed applicators • Creative Paperclay Delight air-dry clay (Red, Yellow, Blue) • Gold rub on paste wax • *Hero Arts* rubber stamps • *Aleene's* (Clear Gel Tacky Glue, 7800 adhesive) • Adhesive Runner • 1¼" Gold bar pin back • Extra strong double-sided Red Liner tape • Gold leafing foil • Adhesive sizing • 3" piece 22 gauge Gold wire • Glass beads • Black paper velvet

INSTRUCTIONS: **Clay:** Blend ½" Yellow, ½" Red and ¼" Blue balls of clay to form Rust. • Color slide mount edges with ink color to match clay. • Apply thin layer of Clear Gel Tacky Glue to front surface. • Roll air dry clay to 1/16" thick and secure to mount. • Stamp texture into clay. Trim clay overlap with scissors. Let dry. • Rub clay surface with metallic paste wax. • **Transparency:** Color tint back of transparency with Pumpkin and Brown ink keeping dragonfly clear. Let dry. • Apply a thin layer of adhesive sizing to back. Let dry. • Press metallic leaf over entire back surface. Burnish gently with fingertip. Fill holes with leaf flakes. Secure transparency behind window of slide mount with Adhesive Runner. • **Beads:** Thread beads on curved wire. Bend wire ends into loops. Secure inside slide mount using strong tape so wire is hidden. • Close slide mount. Cover pin back with velvet paper. Add bar pin.

Collage for an Afternoon

Paris Images

by Mary Kaye Seckler

Looking for a quick project? This one only uses 3 slide mounts. Make it easily in an afternoon.

MATERIALS: 3 *Design Originals* Slide Mounts (#0977 White) • *Jacquard* Lumiere (Purple, Silver Metallic) • 3 large Silver braided jump rings • Silver fleur de lis charm and jump ring • Fibers (Purple, Silver) • Rubber stamps (*Limited Edition "Paris Images"*; *Hero Arts* manuscript background) • Black *Memories* ink • 1/8" Eyelets (3 Silver, 6 Lavender) • Red Liner tape

• 6 antique French postcards • *Kodak* glossy photo paper
INSTRUCTIONS: Reduce and color copy 6 postcards on glossy photo paper. • Paint slide mounts (2 Purple, 1 Silver) with Lumiere paint. Let dry. • Stamp 1 Purple slide mount with "Paris Images". Stamp other slide mounts with Manuscript background. • Tape photos into slide mounts. • Punch three 1/8" holes along side of slide mounts. (A Japanese screw punch is an ideal tool for this job.) Set Lavender eyelets in Purple slide mounts. Set Silver eyelets in Silver slide mount. • Connect with Silver jump rings. Add fibers and fleur charm to rings.

Visit Old Japan with Asian motifs, metal charms, and lush fibers. This is a great book for displaying those vintage photos.

Old Japan

by Mary Kaye Seckler

MATERIALS: 3 *Design Originals* Slide Mounts (#0977 White) • *Jacquard* Lumiere (Green & Copper Metallic) • 3 large Brass braided jump rings • 3 Brass Asian charms and jump rings • Fibers (Orange, Green) • Rubber stamps (*Hero Arts* Chinese newspaper) • Black *Memories* ink • 1/8" eyelets (6 Green, 3 Orange) • Red Liner tape • 6 antique Japanese postcards • *Kodak* glossy photo paper • *Making Memories* metal glue
INSTRUCTIONS: Reduce and color copy 6 postcards on glossy photo paper. • Paint slide mounts (2 Green, 1 Copper) with Lumiere paint. Let dry. • Stamp all 3 slide mounts with Chinese newspaper. • Adhere metal letters to Green slide mount with metal glue. • Tape photos into slide mounts. • Punch three 1/8" holes along side of slide mounts. (A Japanese screw punch is an ideal tool for this job.) Set Green eyelets in Green slide mounts. Set Orange eyelets in Copper slide mount. • Connect with Brass jump rings. Add fibers and charms to rings.

Silver Framed Seashell

by Shirley Rufener

A framed seashell brings the tranquility of the ocean home.

MATERIALS: *Design Originals* Slide Mount (#0975 Large) • *Design Originals* Transparency Sheets (#0562 Nature) • *StazOn* Ink (Timber Brown, Azure, Mustard, Pumpkin) • *Fantastix* applicator (bullet, pointed) • Silver leafing foil • Adhesive sizing • 1/2" wide mounting tape
INSTRUCTIONS: **Transparency**: Apply ink to back of transparency with bullet applicator. Use Mustard and Pumpkin on shell. Shade with Brown. Blend with pointed tip. • Apply Azure near edges of seashell. Let dry. • **Leafing**: Apply thin layer of adhesive sizing to slide mount and transparency. Press metal leaf over surface. Burnish with finger. Press leaf onto bare areas. • Tape transparency inside slide mount. • Display on frame.

Photo Pencil Can
by Babette Cox

Display your family photos or vintage collection on a useful and decorative pencil holder.

MATERIALS: *Design Originals* Heritage Paper (#0411 Letter Postcards) • *Design Originals* Slide Mounts (#0977 White) • *Design Originals* The Ephemera Book (#5207) • Large metal container • Glossy White cardstock • 15 pictures that fit slide mount openings • Red liner tape • *US ArtQuest* Pinata inks (Lime Green, Passion Purple) • Gold *Krylon* marker • Rubbing alcohol • Clothespin • Cosmetic cotton square • Eyedropper • *Aleene's* Tacky Glue • Strong rubber bands • 12" wire 24 gauge • Assorted E-beads • Fibers • Dental floss threader

INSTRUCTIONS: **Frames**: Fold cosmetic cotton square in half and put in clothespin. Squeeze 5 drops of ink of each color onto cotton. Push Gold marker into cotton. Apply to frame with clothespin in swirling manner. Before it dries, drip 4-5 drops of alcohol randomly. Let dry. • Fit frames onto can, trimming as needed, so the can is covered. • Tape pictures to back of frames. • **Can**: Mark the rims with Gold marker. • Bend the frames to lay flat on surface. Adhere frames to can with Red Liner tape, one row at a time, beginning with top. • If you have an empty space on each level, stagger the empty slots with pieces of cardstock. • Hold together with rubber bands a few hours until set. **Finishing**: Glue Letter Postcards paper inside the container. • String beads on 12" wire.

Leafing a Transparency

Set aside. • String beads on fibers using dental floss threader. Tie fibers to wire. • Twist wire in back. Secure with hot glue. • Sign your work.

1. Apply the adhesive sizing to back of color tinted transparency.

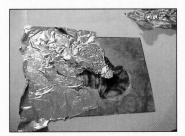

2. Press leaf over surface.

3. Burnish gently with finger. Fill holes with leaf.

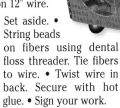

Wish Box
by Babette Cox

Transform an ordinary paper mache box into an inspiring treasure keeper.

MATERIALS: *Design Originals* Heritage Paper (#0410 Seasonal Postcards) • *Design Originals* Slide Mounts (#0979 Round) • *Design Originals* Transparency Sheets (#0556 Word tags) • White cardstock • Paper mache box • *Plaid* Metallic Sequin Black ink • *Chartpak* decorative tape • Black acrylic paint • Sponge brush • Painter's finishing wax • Metal embellishments • Wooden beads • Hot glue • Gold *Krylon* pen • *Aleene's* Tacky Glue • *ColorBox* Chalk pigment (Yellow Cadmium, Olive Pastel, Burnt Sienna, Prussian Blue) • *Ancient Page* (Saffron, Pine, Bordeaux, Cobalt) • Rubber Baby Buggy Bumpers word stamp • Double-stick tape • Sticky note paper

INSTRUCTIONS: **Box**: Paint box with sponge brush using Black acrylic paint. Let dry. • Sparingly rub painter's finishing wax with your finger to the inside crease where lid closes. This will protect the area from sticking together when closed. • Paint wooden beads for feet with Gold pen. Let dry. • **Slide Mounts**: Mask round opening in slide mount with sticky note paper. Add color by tapping chalk pad face down on slide mount (5 Red, 5 Yellow, 4 Blue, 5 Green). Let dry. • Second layer ink: use Saffron on Yellow, Pine on Green, Bordeaux on Red, Cobalt on Blue. • Chalk cardstock squares to put behind slide mounts (2 Yellow, 3 green, 3 red, and 2 blue). Stamp with words. • Edge slide mounts with Gold pen. Glue transparency words with cardstock backing into 10 slide mounts. • Glue images cut from Seasonal Postcards into 9 slide mounts. • **Finishing**: Open lid and lay flat on work surface. Glue slide mounts to top of box. Put a weight on top to secure. Let dry. • Trim slide mounts to fit front and sides of box. Glue in place. • Apply decorative tape to the top and corners. • Hot glue metal embellishments and feet to your box. • Sign your work.

Beaded Edges

1. Fold the tape over edges. Peel liner.

2. Dip the slide mount into the beads.

Fun & Games & Collage

This is the perfect project for flower lovers. These gorgeous blooms from Hawaii lift your spirits. Make this happy project for yourself or for a friend.

Watercolor Effects with Ink

1. Apply ink leaving White area on slide mount.

2. Apply 2nd and 3rd colors randomly.

3. Use brush to remove some ink.

Flowers of Hawaii Accordion Book
by Shirley Rufener

MATERIALS: 6 *Design Originals* Slide Mounts (#0975 Large) • Photos • *StazOn* ink pads (Blazing Red, Ultramarine, Forest Green, Mustard, Pumpkin) • 5 dauber applicators • Large stencil brush • *AMACO* (ArtEmboss medium wt. Pewter metal sheet, WireForm Metal Mesh, Pearlized Gold 24 gauge FunWire) • *Aleene's* 7800 All-Purpose Adhesive • 1/16" hole punch • Gold metallic foil leaf • Leaf adhesive sizing medium • *Xyron* Adhesive Runner • Rubbing alcohol • Poly mallet • Metal letter stamps • Craft foam sheet • 12 small Gold brads • 5 rhinestones • 1 flat button • Thin Gold elastic cord • 16" ribbon 1/2" wide

INSTRUCTIONS: Color slide mounts to coordinate with photos. Apply ink with dauber leaving White areas. Apply second and third color randomly. Immediately stipple with rubbing alcohol. • Press and rotate brush in a spiral to remove some ink. • Color brads with StazOn ink using bullet applicator. To add a second color, gently press brad head directly on ink pad. • Secure brads through 1/16" holes punched in 1 layer of slide mount. Spot leaf selected areas. • **Assembly:** Tape flower photo to each side of slide mount. Lay slide mounts open in a line. Place ribbon across inside of slide mounts leaving 1/4" between each slide mount. Secure ribbon in place. Tape slide mounts shut.

Metal title: Place foil on craft foam over sturdy work surface. Firmly hit metal stamp with mallet. Flatten metal with brayer. Antique metal with StazOn ink using a Fantastix bullet applicator. • Secure to slide mount with 7800. Embellish mounts with curled wire, mesh, buttons and rhinestones using 7800 adhesive. Bind accordion book with a simple gift box style wrapped tie with elastic cord.

Coloring Metal Brads

1. Apply StazOn ink with bullet applicator.

2. Press brad head directly on ink pad.

Stamped Metal Name Plate

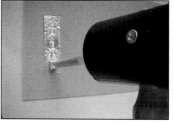

1. Firmly hit stamp with mallet. Flatten with brayer.

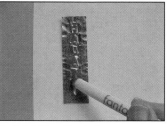

2. Add StazOn ink.

MATERIALS: *Design Originals* Legacy Collage papers (#0530 Mom's Sewing Box, #0546 Currency, #0547 Dictionary, #0555 Tags) • 5 *Design Originals* Slide Mounts (#0978 Black) • *Design Originals* Transparency Sheets (#0556 Word tags, #0559 Alphabet, #0560 Objects) • *Design Originals* The Ephemera Book (#5207 p. 5, 6, 10) • *Stamp In The Hand* Tic Tac Toe Board • Clear acetate • Permanent marker • 2 foam brushes • 4 paper plates • Acrylic paint (Bright Red, Black, White) • Pencil • Scissors • *US ArtQuest* Perfect Paper matte Adhesive (PPA) • E6000 • Cosmetic sponges • *Studio 2* alcohol inks (Real Red, Cactus, Butter Yellow) • *JudiKins* Diamond Glaze • *Brilliance* Galaxy Gold ink pad • *Stampers Anonymous* Crackle Cube stamp • Water-based varnish • Antique Gold Rub 'n Buff • Awl • 2 Gold eye screws • 8" Gold chain

INSTRUCTIONS: Paint Tic Tac Toe Board and edges of game pieces. • Let dry. • Dilute White paint and put wash on board. Let dry. • Dry brush Black on board. • Cut 1⅝" square from acetate and edge with marker. This becomes a template • Place template on Legacy papers. Cut out 9 squares. • Glue with PPA to game tiles. • Glue tiles to board. • Dab Red and Yellow inks onto slide mounts. Let dry. • Cut transparency images. Drip glaze on back. Drip ink onto glaze. Let dry. • Stamp slide mounts with crackle cube. Let dry. Add 1 more application of Red ink. • Glue images in slide mounts. • Cut images from The Ephemera Book and glue to other tiles. • Varnish. Let dry. • Use awl to start holes for eye screws. Add screws and attach chain. • Highlight with Rub 'n Buff.

Tic - Tac - Toe... It's a Winner
by Judy Ross

Even if you don't play Tic-Tac-Toe anymore, you can still have fun with the game board. Turn these squares into art boxes and give yourself a chance to experiment with some new techniques.

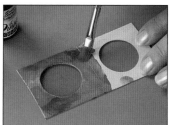

1. Dab inks on slide mounts.

2. Squeeze Diamond Glaze onto back of transparency.

3. Drip the ink onto Diamond Glaze.

4. Add more glaze and another color ink.

Greetings from Carol Wingert! This book was created when a challenge was presented to designers to use slide mounts and transparencies in creative ways. I had wanted to do a travel journal of a recent family vacation to Canada and decided to see how many different uses I could find for these materials in the journal. The slide mounts became title blocks, index dividers and picture frames covered with paint, ink, metal, buttons, photos, hardware and paper clay. The transparencies became titles, index dividers, journaling blocks and inserts behind die-cut numbers. I was very impressed by the versatility of these products!

Canada Travel Journal
by Carol Wingert

MATERIALS: *Anima Designs* (barkskin paper) • *Memory Lane* leather paper for spine • 4 plain kraft colored lunch bags • Sewing machine or Hand sewing tools
INSTRUCTIONS: Lay lunch bags on top of one another, alternating the side of the opening. • Fold all in half. Machine or hand stitch together on the fold line. • The first bag becomes the front and back cover. Wrap it with decorative paper and glue in place. • Add a piece of leather paper to create a spine and machine stitch in place.

Creating the Journal Pages

1. Lay lunch bags alternating open ends.

2. Fold the bags in half.

3. Stitch bags together on fold line.

4. Glue pages to covers.

Travel & Collage

Relive the fun when you preserve memorabilia from your trip. Save the labels from breakfast coffee, clothing, and restaurants. They make delightful additions to your project and invoke happy memories.

1. Cover large slide mount with paper clay. Trim edges and remove center.

2. Stamp images. Let dry.

3. Paint and stain the slide mount.

Cover & Book Construction

MATERIALS: *Design Originals* Slide Mount (#0975 Large) • *Design Originals* Transparency Sheet (#0561 Travels) • *Design Originals* Legacy Collage papers (#0552 Travels, #0541 Report Card) • *Memory Lane* waxed cotton • Rubber Stamps (*Stampa Rosa; Ma Vinci Reliquary; Hero Arts; Denami Design*) • *Creative Paperclay* paper clay • *Plaid* paint and Brown stain • *7 Gypsies* Walnut Ink • *Ranger* Adirondack ink • Glue • Craft knife
INSTRUCTIONS: Add Travels paper to front cover and stamp title. • Cover large slide mount with paper clay. Using craft knife, cut around edges and remove center. Stamp and dry per manufacturer's instructions. • Paint and stain. • Adhere to top of slide mount. • Tape transparency and Report Card paper into slide mount. • Poke holes and thread waxed cotton through slide mount and cover. • Tie knots.

Pages 1 & 2

MATERIALS: *Design Originals* Legacy Collage Paper (#0550 TeaDye Script) • *Design Originals* Slide Mount (#0977 White) • *Design Originals* Transparency Sheet (#0556 Word Tags) • *Design Originals* The Ephemera Book (#5207 p. 15) • Collage papers • *Art Chix* Mini brass tag • Game card • Linen texture rubber stamp • *Li'l Davis Designs* "travels" plaque • *7 Gypsies* bamboo clip • *Ranger* Adirondack ink • Small binder clip • Trip memorabilia • Brown vellum • Waxed linen
INSTRUCTIONS: **p. 1**: Tie metal tag with label to corner of map with waxed linen. Glue map to page. • Glue vellum strip in place. Add photo. Glue labels to page. • **p. 2**: Glue TeaDye Script to page. Add Brass plaque and travel ephemera. • Stamp slide mount with linen textured stamp. Insert transparency and glue to page. • Journal on game card from The Ephemera Book. Insert into lunch bag "pocket" along with tickets and money. • Clip bag closed.

Canadian Travel Journal continued on pages 38 & 39.

A view from up high changes your attitude. Add those breath-taking sights to your journal.

Travel brings you close to wildlife you don't always see. Including all the interesting critters you encountered will make you laugh every time you look at your journal.

Enjoy the people you met along the way. One of the keys to successful travel is appreciating the people who made your visit special. So, get that photo before you depart.

Canada Travel Journal
pages 3-4

by Carol Wingert

MATERIALS: *Design Originals* Legacy Collage Paper (#0550 TeaDye Script) • *Design Originals* Slide Mount (#0975 Large) • *Ink It!* papyrus • *FooFaLa* (hardware, label) • *Nunn Design* (metal circles, hanging charm) • *JudiKins* Toybox stamps • *Ranger* Adirondack Ink • *Coffee Break Design* mini brads
INSTRUCTIONS: **p. 3**: Glue TeaDye Script and papyrus to page. • Add photo. Attach label with brads through one layer of bag. • **p. 4**: Tear, stamp, and glue TeaDye Script to page. • Stamp village scene on both sides of slide mount. Tape photo in slide mount. • Insert computer generated letters into metal circles. Glue to slide mount. • Attach slide mount on page so part hangs over edge of page. Add hardware.

pages 5-6

MATERIALS: *Design Originals* Legacy Collage Paper (#0550 TeaDye Script, #0552 Travels, #0555 Tags) • *Design Originals* Slide Mount (#0979 Round) • *Design Originals* Transparency Sheet (#0558 Script) • *Anima Designs* metal book plate • *Ellison* negative number image die-cut • *7 Gypsies* Walnut ink tags • *Woo Hoo Wowies* charm • *Ranger* ink • Fiber • Office supply date stamp
INSTRUCTIONS: **p. 5**: Glue torn Tags paper to page. • Add photo. • Glue photo and label to tag. Add fibers. Glue to page. • Glue scrap of Travels paper to page. Add book plate with computer generated label.
p. 6: Glue torn TeaDye Script to page. • Add fibers to tag. Glue tag in place. • Add photo. • Ink slide mount with two colors of ink. Insert photo and add charm. Glue to page. • Position transparency behind negative image die-cut. Glue in place.

pages 7-8

MATERIALS: *Design Originals* Legacy Collage Paper (#0555 Tags) • *Design Originals* Transparency Sheet (#0561 Travel) • *Memory Lane* leather paper • *Anima Designs* Bronze mesh • *Making Memories* Metal plates • *Stampington* key • *Coffee Break Designs* Bronze eyelets • *Studio 2* alcohol ink • *Plaid* paint • *Ma Vinci Reliquary* stamps • *Ancient Page* ink • Hemp
INSTRUCTIONS: **p. 7**: Crumple Rust paper. Glue to page. Glue photo in place. • Paint 2 metal plates with acrylic paint. Stamp when dry. Glue to page. Add journaling. • **p. 8**: Cover page with torn Tags paper. Cut out Travel transparency. Ink underside with mustard alcohol ink. Let dry. • Construct pocket of bronze mesh. • Set eyelets and thread hemp. Tie key and transparency to pocket. • Fill pocket with travel memorabilia.

Dream about the beauty you experienced. Better yet, dream of going again. This page will trigger that longing to return.

pages 9-10

MATERIALS: *Design Originals* Legacy Collage Paper (#0540 Skates) • *Design Originals* Slide Mount (#0975 Large, #0978 Black) • *Design Originals* Transparency Sheet (#0556 Word Tags) • *Hillcreek Designs* mini buttons • *Golden* Patina Green glaze • *Inkadinkado* stamp • Ink (*Ranger* Adirondack; *Ancient Page*) • *7 Gypsies* bamboo clip

INSTRUCTIONS: **p. 9**: Stamp "dream" along page border. Glue photo in place. • Paint underside of transparency with Green glaze. Let dry. • Insert into Black slide mount. Add buttons. Glue slide mount to page. • **p. 10**: Glue Skates paper to page. • Lightly ink large slide mount. • Cut out photo index prints. Glue to outside frame of slide mount. Insert photo. • Glue small tag with photo to page corner. Glue slide mount to page. • Insert tickets and travel memorabilia into pockets.

pages 11-12

MATERIALS: Design Originals Slide Mount (#0977 White) • *Design Originals* Transparency Sheet (#0556 Word Tags) • *Making Memories* word definition sheet • *3M* ink jet acetate transparency • Tiny clear glass beads • Double-sided tape • *Xyron* adhesive

INSTRUCTIONS: *Note: Do not make p. 12 until you sew pocket on p. 13.* **p. 11**: Glue photos and travel ephemera to page. Journal under photo. Add "remember" transparency. • **p. 12**: Cut small slide mount in half. Ink frame. Insert transparency "Adventure". Glue to bottom of page to act as index divider. • Cover page with aged paper. Glue photo on page. • Computer generate text "Fresh glacier water" on acetate transparency, spaced around photos. Attach acetate to page with Xyron adhesive. • Adhere clear beads to page bottom with double sided tape.

Life is full of unique and unforgettable experiences. A photo can't capture how cold the water was or how exhilarating it was to touch. But with this page, you will remember it all, right down to the crunching sound of the snow beneath your boots.

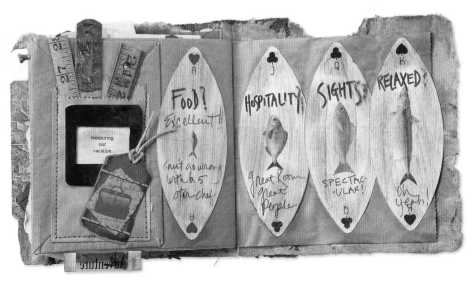

pages 13-14

MATERIALS: *Design Originals* Slide Mount (#0978 Black) • *Nostalgiques* tape measure stickers • *Karen Foster Design* travel sticker • *7 Gypsies* Walnut ink tag • *Plaid* Brown stain • Playing cards • Hemp

INSTRUCTIONS: Make a Brown paper pocket. Sew to page. • Insert computer generated text into Black slide mount. • Add to page with travel related ephemera. • Stain playing cards with Brown stain and add handwritten journaling. • Adhere to pages.

The last page of your book summarizes your trip. Put your best thoughts here. Take measure of your experience and consider how it has added to your life.

Windows and Walls

by Mary Kaye Seckler

Play with a variety of themes when you make this trendy tag book. It is full of slide mount windows that let you see the charms on the next page.

BASIC MATERIALS: *Design Originals* Slide Mounts (Three #0977 White, Six #0979 Round) • 1/8" Red Liner Tape • *3M* double-stick mounting tape • *Marvy* stamp pads (#18 Brown, #36 Crimson) • Craft knife • Charms (lock, key, music, dragonfly, Asian, French) • Brass brads • Fibers • Acetate • Instant coffee • Torn scrap beige tissue • *All Night Media* Fleur de lis punch • Hole punches (swirl, dragonfly) • Stamp motifs (keys, locks, music, dragonfly, words, Asian, French) • Scraps of text and sheet music • French postage stamps

PREPARATION: **Coffee Dye**: Dab strong coffee on all tags and slide mounts. Sprinkle instant coffee crystals to create areas of deeper color. Let dry. • Cut all slide mounts apart.

COVER MATERIALS: *Design Originals* Legacy Paper (#0498 TeaDye Tapestry) • *7 Gypsies* tag book • 3 White 1" tags • Three 1/8" eyelets • Small spiral punch • Gold leaf • Ribbon • Gold metallic thread • Watch parts • *ColorBox* Chestnut Cat's Eye ink • *Making Memories* metal glue • *Missing Link* alphabet stamps

INSTRUCTIONS: **Book Cover**: Remove covers and pages from spirals. Glue TeaDye Tapestry paper to front and back covers. • **Front Cover Art**: Cut dyed slide mounts in half. Edge sides with Chestnut ink. • Edge tags too. • Remove strings from tags. Set eyelets in tags. Reattach strings. •

Apply Gold leaf to one tag and punch spiral. • Tape ribbon around second tag. Add 2 small cross-stitches using Gold thread. • Glue watch parts onto third tag with metal glue. • Tape strings inside slide mounts. Trim excess string. Use mounting tape to adhere top slide mount to bottom, enclosing tag. Stamp 'Windows and Walls' on front cover. • **Back Cover**: Stamp round slide mount with pattern. Stamp signature on back cover. Place slide mount over signature stamp. Glue to cover. • **Assembly**: When covers and pages are finished, reattach spiral.

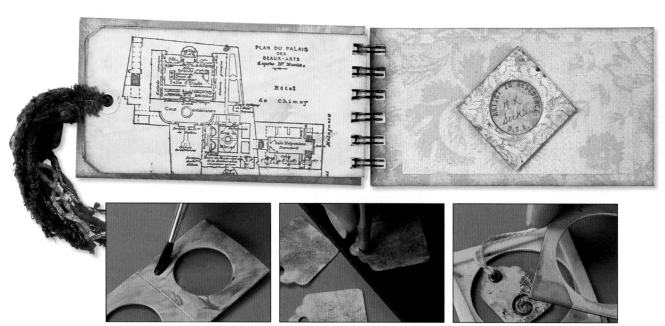

1. Coffee dye coin holders and tags.

2. Add eyelets to tag.

3. Sandwich tag between slide mount pieces.

Themes in Collage

Tag Art Pages: Each segment consists of one window page and one wall page and has its own theme.

Page Construction: *All stamps done in Brown ink unless stated otherwise.* Stamp slide mount. • Place on first tag. Trace opening onto tag and cut out with craft knife. Line up tags and trace slide opening onto second tag lightly in pencil. Cover both slide holes with acetate using double-stick tape. Follow directions for decorating tag. Tape slide mount halves on each side of hole using mounting tape. Attach fibers to tags.

#1 Locks and Keys: Stamp baroque pattern on Beige tissue scrap. Glue to first tag. • Follow Page Construction steps. • Stamp lock and key images on both sides of both tags. Attach lock and key charms to second page and erase the pencil lines.

#2 Music: Stamp round slide mount with script. Glue music scrap to first tag. • Follow Page Construction steps. • Stamp music motifs. Attach music charm to second tag.

#3 Dragonfly: Stamp swirl onto slide mount. • Glue text scrap to first tag. • Punch swirl and dragonfly in first tag.• Follow Page Construction steps. • Stamp dragonfly stamps on both tags. Attach dragonfly charm to second tag and erase pencil lines.

#4 Asian: Stamp round slide mount with Asian script. • Stamp Asian script and glue to first tag. • Follow Page Construction steps. • Stamp Asian motifs. Stamp chops in red. Attach Asian charm to second tag and erase pencil lines.

#5 French: Stamp pattern onto slide mount. • Glue French text scrap to first tag. • Follow Page Construction steps. • Glue French postage stamps in place. • Stamp French motifs on both tags. Attach Fleur de lis charm to second tag and erase pencil lines.

Pendants

by Jana Ewy

Make a zany name plate to wear next time you go to a craft show. These eyecatchers are sure to get noticed.

BASIC MATERIALS: *Design Originals* Legacy Collage Paper (0547 Dictionary) • *Design Originals* Slide Mounts (#0977 White, #0978 Black, #0979 Round) • *Design Originals* Transparency Sheet (#0559 Alphabet) • Acetate • *AMACO* (ArtEmboss Extra soft embossing sheets-Copper, Gold, Pewter; Metal stamp art inks-Rust, Black; 1/16" WireForm armature wire) • Gold beading wire • Gold 24 gauge wire • *StazOn* ink (Brown, Red) • Craft knife • Black acrylic paint • Heat gun • Hole punch (1/4", 11/4") • Scissors • Assorted beads • Alphabet stickers • Letters cut from magazine • Watch parts • Sticky dots • Double-sided tape • Glue stick • Heat gun • *PSX* Butterfly rub-on • *Making Memories* Letter "B" • Eyelets • Eyelet setter • Needle tool • Rubber mallet • Hammer • 2" circle template • Black acrylic paint • Paper scrap • Rubber stamp • Beaded fringe

BASIC INSTRUCTIONS:
Color metal sheet: Apply inks. Heat set. • Crumple sheets and flatten.
Texture metal sheet: Hammer with rubber mallet. Rub with Black acrylic paint if desired.
Covering Slide Mounts: Cut sheets slightly larger than slide mount. Apply sticky dots to slide mount and cover with metal. Wrap metal around mount. Secure on inside with glue. Cut out one window by making an "X" and folding metal to inside. Trim so there is no overlap.

Transparency Window: Cut transparency and collage paper slightly larger than window. • Assemble assorted letters to spell out name. Adhere letters to collage paper making sure they fit within window.
Scroll: Make scroll shape with armature wire. Hammer to flatten. Position scroll pieces on slide mount. Use needle tool to punch holes where needed for securing. Stitch through holes with beading wire to secure into place. Attach pendant to cord.

Kathy

INSTRUCTIONS: Color and texture metal embossing sheet. • Cover slide mount. Prepare transparency window. • Apply butterfly rub-on. Follow scroll directions.

Jana

INSTRUCTIONS: Trace 2" circle on round slide mount using template. Cut out. • Texture 21/2" x 41/2" pewter rectangle. • Punch out 11/4" circle at one end of rectangle. • Glue on small watch parts. Position paper and transparency inside mount and seal closed. • Use needle tool to punch holes around slide mount. Stitch on beads with beading wire. Punch two holes at top and attach eyelets. Attach pendant to cord.

Barbara

INSTRUCTIONS: Color and crumple metal sheet. • Prepare transparency window. • Tape paper and transparency into slide mount. • Apply butterfly rub-on. • Follow scroll directions. Add letter "B" to scroll.

Kenny

INSTRUCTIONS: Texture 11/2" square of pewter. • Follow transparency window directions. Tape pewter and transparency into slide mount. • Follow scroll directions. • Punch hole at bottom of slide mount and attach eyelet. Secure a string of beads from eyelet to scroll work. Attach pendant to cord.

Suzanne

INSTRUCTIONS: Color and texture metal sheet. • Cover slide mount with metal. Prepare transparency window. • Cut beaded fringe. Glue to bottom of slide mount. Position transparency and paper inside mount and tape closed. Follow Scroll directions. • Punch two holes at top and attach eyelets. Attach pendant to cord.

1. Cover slide mount with foil.

2. Punch out letters.

3. Curl end of wire.

4. Flatten wire with hammer.

5. Punch holes in slide.

6. Wire metal to slide.

Dressed-Up Collage

A B C Book

Make a unique book of slide mounts containing wire mesh with charms. Or make an easier project using transparencies. Both projects are a lot of fun.

1. Color foil

2. Smooth crumpled foil.

3. Remove center.

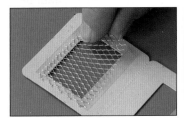

4. Glue mesh.

MATERIALS: *Design Originals* Slide Mounts (#0977 White) • *Design Originals* Transparency Sheet (#0559 Alphabet) • *AMACO* ArtEmboss light wt. Gold embossing sheets; WireForm 1/16" aluminum armature wire; Black metal stamp art ink) • Gold beading wire • Metal alphabet stamps • *Pinata* inks (Magenta, Yellow) • Craft knife • Black acrylic paint • Heat gun • Hole punch (1/16", 1/2" circle, square) • Scissors • Game tiles • Sticky dots • Double-sided tape • Glue stick

INSTRUCTIONS: Color front and back of 3 Gold soft metal embossing sheets with Pinata inks. Heat set the inks. Crumple sheets and flatten. • Cut sheets slightly larger than slide mount. Apply sticky dots to three slide mounts and cover with metal. Cut out window by making an "X" and folding metal to inside. Trim so there is no overlap. Cut transparencies A, B, C, D, E. • Position B, C, and D inside mount, securing with glue. • Apply glue or tape to inside of mount. Slide over the accordion pleats before sealing completely. Repeat with the other two mounts. • **Book Cover:** Apply sticky dots to two slide mounts and cover with metal. Cut out only one window on each mount. Position and glue transparency A and E behind the window opening. • Apply glue or tape to inside of mount. Slide over front and back tabs before sealing completely. • Cut a 1" x 2" piece of metal, apply tape to back and adhere over spine, overlapping the front and back covers. • Embellish with metal stamped letters, game tiles and wire.

Unlock Your Mind
by Jana Ewy

MATERIALS: *Design Originals* Legacy Collage paper (0547 Dictionary) • *Design Originals* Slide Mounts (#0977 White) • *Design Originals* Transparency Sheet (#0560 Objects) • *AMACO* (ArtEmboss Extra soft embossing sheets-light Copper, light Aluminum; WireForm Copper impression mesh; Metal stamp art inks-Black, Rust) • 24 gauge Gold wire • 22 gauge Copper wire • Gold beading wire • Metal alphabet stamps • *Acey Deucy* Legatoria rubber stamp • Brown *StazOn* ink • Craft knife • Black acrylic paint • Heat gun • Hole punches (1/16", 1/8") • Charms • Assorted beads • Sticky dots • Double-sided tape • Glue stick

INSTRUCTIONS: Cut a 2" x 5 1/2" strip of Dictionary paper. Use grid pattern on back to measure 2" from each end. Score down each of the seven remaining lines. Accordion fold along score lines. • Color two Gold soft metal embossing sheets with Rust and Brown inks. Heat set inks. Crumple sheets and flatten out. • Cut sheets slightly larger than slide mount. Apply sticky dots to 3 slide mounts. Cover with metal. Cut an "X" in window and fold metal to inside. Trim so there is no overlap. • Cut mesh to size and tape inside slide mount. • Slide over the accordion pleats before sealing completely. Repeat with other two mounts. • **Book Cover**: Cut two 2 1/2" squares of Copper. Rubber stamp and heat set ink. Continue to heat until copper begins to change color. Let cool. • Cut slide mount in half. • Apply sticky dots to each half. Cover with copper. Trim copper to size or fold to inside of slide mount. • Cut out transparency and position image in window.

5. Close slide mount onto accordion fold.

6. Glue paper over spine.

Secure with glue. • Cut two 1 1/2" squares of Dictionary paper. Glue one behind transparency and the other over window on back cover. Cut 1" x 2" Dictionary paper. Glue over spine. Glue on front and back covers. Trim corners if necessary. Embellish with stamped words, wire, beads and charms.

Make a card that will survive the test of time. Collage on textured Copper for a surprisingly different card medium.

Butterfly Cards

MATERIALS: *Design Originals* Slide Mounts (#0975 Large) • *Design Originals* Legacy Collage paper (0547 Dictionary) • *AMACO* (WireForm Copper impression mesh; ArtEmboss Copper medium wt. Embossing sheets; Rust metal stamp art ink) • *PSX* butterfly rub-ons • *Fiskars* deckle scissor • Brown *StazOn* ink • Brown *ColorBox* pigment ink • Craft knife • Heat gun • 1/8" hole punch • Metal eyelets • Assorted alphabet stickers • Double-sided tape • Textured rubber mallet • Cardstock • Decorative corner punch • Sharp craft knife

GENERAL INSTRUCTIONS: Cut two 5" x 6" rectangles of Copper. • Cut slide mount in half. Color metal and slide mounts with inks. Heat set. • Texture metal with rubber mallet. • Mark hole placement along one side 3/4" from top, 3" center, and 3/4" from bottom. Punch holes. • Use holes as guide to punch second sheet. • Trim top sheet with deckle scissors for card front. • **Hinges:** Cut three 1" x 3" strips of Dictionary paper and cardstock. Glue together. Score center of each and fold in half. Punch both ends of strip with decorative corner punch. Position over holes along card spine. Set eyelets. • **Front:** Place slide mount slightly off center. Trace inside opening and cut out with a sharp craft knife. Cut Copper mesh just larger than opening. • Adhere mesh inside slide mount with tape. Attach with eyelets. **Inside:** Tape other slide mount over opening on inside of card. Adhere butterfly rub-ons so they appear through window.

Butterflies Are Free

Follow General Instructions. Embellish card front with the alphabet stickers.

Butterflies Flutter By

Follow General Instructions. Embellish card front by stamping out the words BUTTERFLIES and BY. Rub over stamped letters with Black acrylic paint. Use alphabet stickers to spell FLUTTER.

Suzanne Card

MATERIALS: *Design Originals* Legacy Collage paper (0526 Two Ladies) • *Design Originals* Slide Mounts (#0979 Round) • *Design Originals* Transparency Sheet (#0559 Alphabet) • 6" x 10" cardstock • *AMACO* (ArtEmboss light wt. Copper embossing metal sheet; WireForm 1/16" armature wire; Rust metal stamp art ink) • *StazOn* Brown ink • *ColorBox* pigment ink (Brown, Terra cotta) • Craft knife • Round hole punch (1/8", 11/4") • Eyelets • Eyelet setter • Alphabet letters • Game piece • Charms • Itty Bitty gold beads • Glitter • Black acrylic paint • Silver brads • Metal alphabet stamps • Hammer • Sticky dots • Double-sided tape • Glue stick

INSTRUCTIONS: **Card:** Glue Two Ladies paper to cardstock. Score center. Fold in half. • Tear and ink card edge with pigment inks. Punch out two 11/4" circles. • **Copper frames:** Cut two Copper 21/2" squares. Hammer to texture. Apply inks to distress. • Punch a 11/4" circle in center of each. • **S frame:** Cut round slide mount apart. Cut each piece into 13/4" circle • Cover one with Copper. • Tape "S" transparency inside the covered slide mount window. Glue over hole in card front. Glue other slide mount inside card. • **Square frame:** Form a small spiral with armature wire. Hammer to flatten. Place spiral, gold beads and glitter in slide mount. Glue shut. Cover with copper. Miter corners and fold to back. • Stamp name on all four sides as shown. Rub with Black acrylic paint to highlight letters. Align over second cut out in card front. Punch holes and adhere with brads. • Embellish with stickers, game pieces, charms.

Tip
Place dots of hot glue on one side of a mallet to make a texturing tool.

Copper & Collage

by Jana Ewy

Hammered Copper covered slide mounts give this card a metallic sparkle and an element from nature. Try adding buttons with wire for a different look. Fun game pieces and charms give these cards appeal.

1. Texture with hammer.

2. Heat to change color.

3. Trim corners.

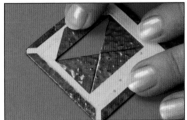

4. Cut "x". Fold around.

BASIC MATERIALS: *Design Originals* Legacy Collage paper (0526 Two Ladies, 0542 Father's Farm) • *Design Originals* Slide Mounts (#0977 White) • *Design Originals* Transparency Sheet (#0556 Word Tags, #0558 Script, #0561 Travel) • 6" x 10" cardstock • *AMACO (*ArtEmboss light wt. Copper embossing metal sheets; Rust metal stamp art ink; Copper WireMesh) • Gold beading wire • *StazOn* Brown ink • *ColorBox* pigment ink (Brown, Terra cotta) • Craft knife • Hole punch ($1/8$", $1/16$") • Eyelets • Eyelet setter • Alphabet letters • Buttons • Small Gold screws • Game pieces • Charms • Jump rings • Black acrylic paint • Metal alphabet stamps • Hammer • Sticky dots • Double-sided tape • Glue stick

BASIC INSTRUCTIONS:
Glue collage paper to cardstock • Score. Fold in half. Ink edges with Brown pigment ink. Cut a $2^1/2$" piece of Copper. Hammer to texture. Apply inks to give distressed look. Cut slide mount in half and cover one half with Copper. • Cut out window by making an "X" and folding metal to inside. Trim so there is no overlap. Position slide mount on card front, trace inside window. Cut out with craft knife.

Home Sweet Home

Punch holes in bottom of Copper slide mount. Thread small tags through holes. Add small bead. Tie knot. • Tape HOME transparency into Copper slide mount. • Tape newspaper inside card behind window. • Tape slide mounts to both sides of card. Set eyelets. • Attach Family transparency on card with eyelets. Punch around card and stitch with beading wire. Embellish with Alphabet stickers and buttons.

Hope and Dream

Punch holes in bottom of Copper slide mount. Add charms with jump rings. • Tape "Believe" transparency to Copper slide mount. Cut wire mesh. Place it inside card behind window. • Tape slide mounts to both sides of card front. Set eyelets. Attach "Dream" transparency with eyelets. • Embellish with Alphabet stickers and game pieces.

Documents

Follow Basic Instructions for making card. • Place scrap paper behind transparency inside card behind window. • Tape slide mount to both sides of card front. Set eyelets. Attach other transparencies on card with eyelets. Embellish with Alphabet stickers and game pieces.

Slide Mount Booklet with Collage

Wistful vintage baby photo gives a dreamy quality to this wonderful page.

Recapture an innocent age when we could sit on a blanket in the front yard and play in the sun all day.

Remember when children played outside and your best friend lived next door? Don't you wish life was that simple now? Bring back those memories with this lovely page.

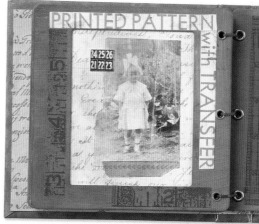

Ever wonder how we moved from dolls and carriages to video games? This page holds a happy reminiscence of a time gone by.

These girls are all dressed up in their Sunday best, polished shoes and hair bows.

Remember the friends on your block, or place an old family photo to show your children what their great grandparents were like when they were young.

Show off your collection of photos with this book made of slide mounts held together with a simple binding technique.

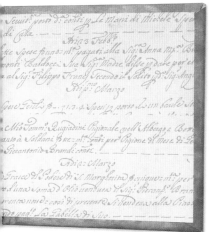

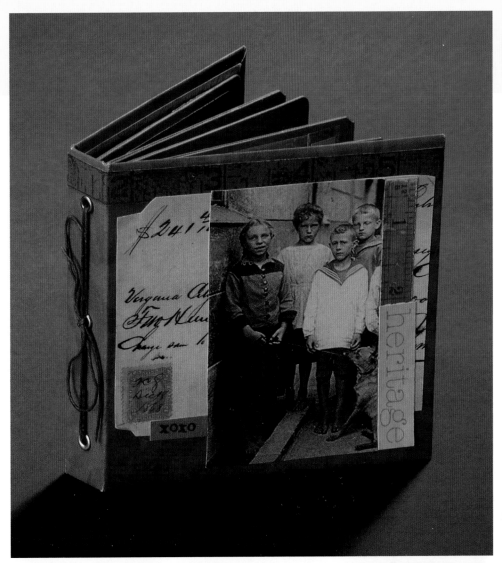

1. Attach the eyelet to slide mount with tool.

2. Thread through center hole of each slide mount.

3. Bring thread out through center hole.

Heritage Book
by Renée Plains

Easy Binding Technique

Make an Overhand Knot. Tie Bow.

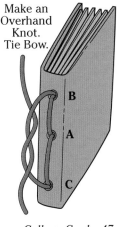

MATERIALS: *Design Originals* Legacy Collage Paper (#0530 Mom's Sewing Box, #0541 Report Card, #0547 Dictionary, #0550 TeaDye Script, #0551 Legacy Words, #0490 Coffee Linen, #0493 Brown Linen, #0495 Brown Floral) • *Design Originals* Slide Mounts (#0975 Large) • 3¾" x 8⅛" cardboard • *Limited Edition* rulers collage sheet • *Tracy Roos* photo sheet • 18 eyelets • 24" Waxed linen string

INSTRUCTIONS: **Slide mounts:** Cover 5 slide mounts with Coffee Linen paper. • Stamp different rulers on Brown Linen paper. Glue border of stamped rulers and rulers from Mom's Sewing Box paper on each slide mount. • Glue photos in each frame. • Collage each picture with elements and words from Legacy Collage papers. • Punch matching sets of 3 holes in each slide mount. Set eyelets. • **Make cover:** Score cardboard 3¾" from each side, making ⅝" spine. Glue Brown Floral paper to cover, overlapping and folding to inside. Glue TeaDye Script paper inside cover. • **Binding:** Punch holes in cover lining up with holes in slide mount. • Thread waxed linen through center holes in slide mounts. Even thread ends. Push both ends through center hole A in cover. • Split threads apart. Thread one string through cover at B, through slide mount holes, and back out B. • Repeat process at C with other end of string. • Tie ends in bow.

Embellishing with Collage

Purchasing a ready-made book jump starts your project. Now you can focus on the fun part-embellishing the cover and pages.

Journey Accordion Book

by Shannon Smith

MATERIALS: *Design Originals* Legacy Collage Papers (#0480 Green Floral, #0487 Rust Linen, #0490 Coffee Linen) • Images from *Design Originals* The Ephemera Book (#5207, p. 7, 20, 21, 23) • *Design Originals* Slide Mounts (#0977 White, #0975 Large) • *Design Originals* Transparency Sheets (#0556 Word Tags, #0558 Script, #0559 Alphabet) • Cardstock (Celery Green, Autumn Gold, Burgundy) • *Kolo* accordion album • *Stampa Rosa* Fresco ink pads • *Making Memories* tags • Gold filigree corner mount • *Adornaments* fibers • Plastic wrap • Adhesive
INSTRUCTIONS: For slide mount on cover of book, use a crumpled piece of plastic wrap. Dab on ink pad, then onto slide mount for a crackled effect. Repeat with a different color. For other slide mounts, pat the ink directly onto the slide mount with a Fresco ink pad. The linen texture of the ink pad will transfer to the slide mount for a linen effect. Mat images with cardstock and adhere to pages. Mount transparencies in slide mounts, using cardstock mats if desired. Glue elements to cover and pages of journal.

1. Dab the Pink ink onto large slide mount.

2. Repeat step 1 using the Yellow ink.

3. Color a small slide mount with Yellow.

4. Press Pink Fresco ink over Yellow for linen look.